# THE PRODUCTION ASSISTANT'S HANDBOOK

by
**Jeff Alves**

Foreword
**William-Alan Landes**

**PLAYERS PRESS**

Library of Congress Cataloging-in-Publication Data

Alves, Jeff.
    The production assistant's handbook / by Jeff Alves ; edited and foreword by William-Alan Landes.
      p. cm.
      ISBN 0-88734-958-7 (alk. paper)
      1. Motion pictures--Production and direction--Handbooks, manuals, etc. 2. Motion pictures--Production and direction--Vocational guidance. I. Landes, William-Alan. II. Title.

PN1995.9.P7A475 2004
791.4302'32--dc22
                                                        2004058676

# FOREWORD

There are numerous books about the glamour of the entertainment industry: stars abound, the rich and famous are everywhere. We all seem to enter the industry blinded by stardust, armed with misconceptions and driven by youthful overconfidence. It's a beautiful dream. I did it just this way. I finished school and headed to the West Coast from New York; I was confident that anything I hadn't learned would be of minimal importance and that on the set and in the screening room I'd pick it all up.

It was never that easy. Over the years, again and again, I've heard "my story" from the famous and forgotten, whether actor, director, technician or crew member. We each seem to learn, sometimes too late, that there is more to know than we have learned. The difficult part is where to find this information.

There are very few good books that meticulously outline the specifics accurate and realistically on what really is necessary to fulfill and acquire specific jobs within the industry. There are even fewer books that bridge the gap of formal education and professional training. Whether you consider the Production Assistant position as a starting or entry job, a stepping stone up the production ladder to director or producer, important career within the production community, this book has the information you need.

Jeff Alves, formerly a production assistant/coordinator, currently owner of 24/7 Production Communication Rentals, a rental house in Hollywood, California who carefully documented his learning experiences, has truly brought a greater clarity to one of the significant areas of the entertainment industry. His book not only details the starting how-to for Production Assistants but it is a continual working handbook that everyone working on or in a production should read and re-read. The information outstrips just the Production Assistant; it is an invaluable reference for Production Manager, Stage Manager, Producer, Director and even Actor. It guides you through the myriad of mazes within the industry and clearly outlines, in detail, the working production from start to finish.

I remember working for Marvin Miller and we had a star actor who was late several times. Mr. Miller told me, "Look, kid. It doesn't matter how talented you are, in this business you need to show up on time and do your job." That remains one of the most useful pieces of information I ever learned on a set. It when emphasized when Mr. Miller closed the production because the star was late too often. The film was later completed but with a different star.

In the days when I first worked production, I would have given anything to have had the information Jeff has carefully presented in this book. Working with this material took me back to when I hired and worked with neophytes, of which I wasn't much more. Boy, how many questions and problems, my own included, could have been avoided had they or I read this text. Many of the people I encountered and have known might have survived the industry pitfalls and even achieved their goals or dreams, if only they had read this guide.

—William-Alan Landes

# CONTENTS

# PART FOUR
## ~Duties of a Production Assistant~



# PART FIVE
## ~Stage Versus Location~



# PART SIX
## ~Money Matters~

This is dedicated to my beautiful wife, Blanca and our first child Isabel. Thanks for giving me the love and strength to pursue my dreams and for believing in my potential.

Jeff

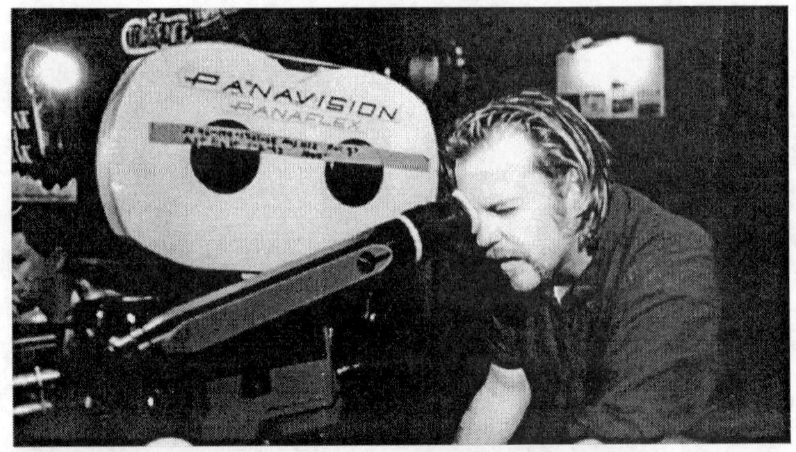

© Showtime Networks, Inc. (Top) First-time director Kiefer Sutherland checks out the film action for the Showtime original movie LAST NIGHT. (Bottom) A scene from the movie in which Sutherland plays a death-row prisoner receiving a final visit from his sister, played by Amanda Plummer. *Photo courtesy of Showtime Networks, Inc.*

# Introduction

The entertainment industry is one of the largest— and fastest growing —— occupational fields in the world. TV and movie production companies are constantly seeking dedicated, motivated Production Assistants to enter this field. Once you have joined the fellowship of entertainment professionals, you can advance as far as your skills and knowledge will take you. This book reveals everything you need to know about becoming and being an excellent Production Assistant.

When I first started no one warned me that I needed to know both how to get a job, and, how to do it well once I got it. Since then, I haved learned many strategies for doing this highly detailed work. Before this book was published, the only way to learn these strategies was through on-the-job training that involved **much** frustration and anguish due to **wasted** effort and many mistakes.

Exactly what is a Production Assistant, and what does a production assistant do? This book will fully describe the important role of a Production Assistant in film or television. It takes you step by step through the various duties , from start to finish.

Getting started in the industry can be very difficult. The old adage about "who you know" is very apropos. If you know the right people you can quickly get a job. Can you keep it ? Will you get hired again? The answer to these questions will depend on your performance and abilities. You can know the Producer; get hired ; do a poor job and out you go. Who you know *is* important, but what you know may be more important.

If you're starting out, and don't have a "who" connection to get you that first job, how do you land it ? What you know will help, not only to make the right contacts, but also to make the contacts work to your advantage. One thing that I thought should weigh heavily would be a good film education. Now, I'm totally in favor of education ; unfortunately the classes are great for theory and techniques but no help learning the *ins* and *outs* of being on a professional production set or out on location.

The information you can learn from this book was learned by me the hard way ; long hours, good and bad experiences and by observing mistakes, my own and those of others. Despite these trials and tribulations, I passionately enjoy my work and highly recommend it to you. It has exposed me to many kinds of people and many areas of expertise in television, commercials, video and film production. I hope that this book encourages you to reap the same satisfaction in your entertainment career.

The tips and techniques I learned are offered here to help you move through the production maze. Hopefully the information presented will give you the edge needed to start working as a Production Assistant. Hard work combined with the knowledge of what is expected of you can open the door to many opportunities in this exciting industry. You can look at being a PA as a career in itself or as an entry level job that will start you on your way to a more specific crew position or to the stellar heights of Producer or Director.

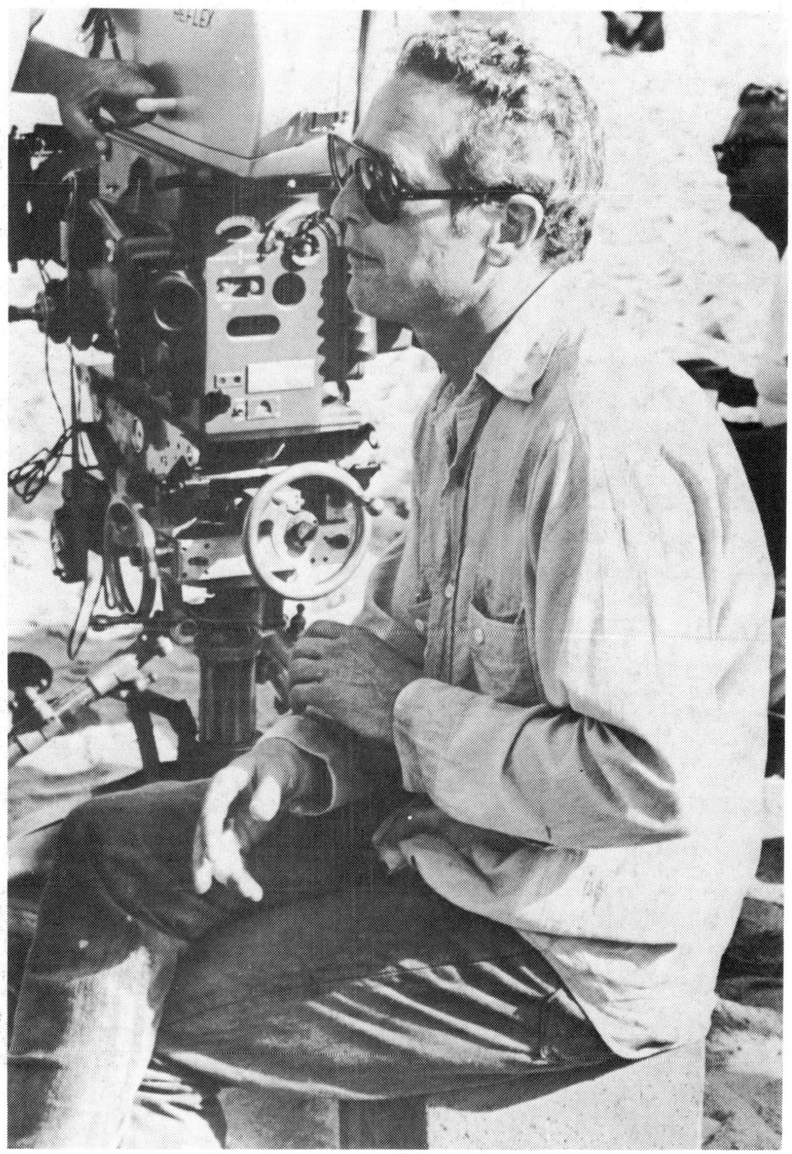

© Universal Pictures - Paul Newman directing NEVER GIVE AN INCH. *Courtesy of Universal Studios.*

© Universal City Studios, Inc. Ron Howard directing PARENTHOOD. *Courtesy of Universal Studios.*

# PART ONE
## ~Starting Out~

Paramount Pictures and its beautiful arches is a fixture in Hollywood, Calif.

The Walt Disney Company headquarters are located in Burbank, Calif., and is a must see for its beautifully colored statues of the seven dwarfs in its structure.

# CHAPTER 1

## Finding A Job:
## Who, What & Where to Look

The most important factor in getting a Production Assistant (PA) job is looking in the right place. Of the several ways to become a PA, the easiest is to know someone who is hiring a PA. The next best someone is a working PA. As I've stated, having a contact in the business is the quickest and surest way to get your start. Where you go from there is up to you.

Another way is to send your resume to a production house. This is a competitive business, and production houses welcome a resume from a hard-working, motivated self-starter. If you have prior experience, a resume can be a helpful way of communicating that to your interviewer. If you send a resume, be sure to include a well-written, enthusiastic cover letter.

A resume, however is not essential to landing a job as a PA. One approach that works well is to walk directly into the office of a production company and to ask to speak with the person in charge of hiring Production Assistants. In large companies, the Production Coordinator or Producer or Associate Producer may do the hiring. In some companies, the in-house Coordinator may freelance or work out of another location. Therefore, when you ask to speak with the coordinator about seeking employment, you may be told that the coordinator is not in the office. The main object is to be in the right place at the right time.

One way to meet the right people is to go to some working stages and to inquire about jobs there. This is a very delicate business, so use common sense when approaching a Coordinator or anyone who is busy working. Remember that first impressions are important. Most companies hire freelance crews for upcoming jobs. Freelance employees do not have permanent staff positions. Many periodicals and trade papers include prospective freelance PA jobs. It only takes a phone call to inquire about an available position.

Don't hesitate to take any work that is offered to you. What you need is experience, and one way to get it may by working for free. Sometimes, freebies (or "Spec", as it is called) offer free "on the job training", which can help you gain experience. Though this training period is not easy, if you are committed to finding a job and are just starting out, it is an option that could be worth your time.

Inquiring about jobs also offers additional payoffs. Even if a company doesn't need anyone at this time, they may put you on a future call list to refer you to someone else who has work available. Your ultimate goal is to obtain as many names and contacts as possible. Let everybody know that you want to become a PA. You never know who you're going to meet or when you're going to meet someone who can help you.

Another way of finding a job is to look in your area's film and video production directory. *Directories are an excellent source of information concerning production companies. Call the companies you think you might like to work for. Most companies will curtly suggest that you send a resume and then quickly hang up. Send it. After sending your resume, always follow up with a phone call.

Keep a written log of who you spoke to, interviews, where and when you sent each resume, etc. Follow up with Thank You cards if someone is helpful, notes and cards that you are working; even holiday cards to help them remember you.

When you get that interview, make sure the person interviewing you knows as much about you and your background as possible. Highlight special skills and knowledge you have: you were a waiter, teacher, cab driver; each of these and other skills have a special importance to a production. If you have lived in the area where the company is shooting, your familiarity with the neighborhood could be an asset; you'll know the streets and save time on errands. If you have a pick-up truck or large vehicle mention it—it's an important item that could help get you that job.

The last way is through the internet. Since the explosion of the internet information has been accessible world wide. More and more film companies, production houses, rental houses, etc., have put up their web sites. This gives you precise information on what, where, and when they are looking for PA's and other crew members for hire. Knowledge and information are power, so search and search the film industry sites for work.  Here are a few of the better æsites:
     productionhub.com
     crewnet.com
     mandy.com
     hollywood911.com
     indiehub.com

media-match.com
shoots.com

Don't forget about those film industry trade papers like Variety and Backstage for job hunting also.

Give 110% of your effort, and show prospective employers that you are looking for a company that likes that attitude. This is a high-energy business. When speaking with people, show your enthusiasm!

*The LA411 in the Los Angeles area.
*The Creative Industry Handbook in the Los Angeles area.
*The Reel Directory in the San Francisco area.
*The NY411 in the New York area.
*The Not For Tourists Guide - Los Angeles,Chicago, New York

# CHAPTER 2

## Four Kinds of Assignments: Booked/On Hold/Half Day/ Specs & Freebies

"Booked"

The goal of your first job-seeking efforts is to be "booked", which means that the Coordinator has hired you for a certain number of days (that is, the number of days you and the Coordinator discussed). If you are booked, you can count on actually getting the job 99% of the time. The production assignment has been awarded to the Director, and the wheels are in motion to begin the production. The other 1% allows for the slim chance that the company's production job might not work out. If the job offer falls through, it is usually due to some sort of problem between the advertising company and the clients' producer or with the production company that has hired you. This seldom happens once you have been booked.

## "On Hold"

Sometimes however, the company is less certain of getting a job. Nonetheless, when you are put "on hold", the company is likely to get the job. Being "on hold" means that if the company is awarded the job, the Coordinator will use you. No guarantees come with this. Being put "on hold" is both good and bad. The good aspects are that the company wants to hire you and you might have work lined up if the company secures the job. However, there is still the possibility the job might fall through.

There are many problems with being "on hold". You could accept the "on hold" status and then another job comes through. You might find out about a job, after you accepted "on hold". Do you except? Can you book it? You might be offered a job that overlaps or conflicts with the "on hold" job.

I don't believe there is any one simple answer to the above problems. Each problem can have many solutions. Unfortunately the bottom line is that you may have to pass on a good job, only to find out that the "on hold" job doesn't materialize. I recommend going after all possible jobs; then if you book a conflict, tell both parties about the situation. Usually industry professionals will understand that a booking is better than a maybe. The real dilemma is if the "on hold" is a big job and the booking a small one; that's a decision you'll have to make on your own—wait and take a chance or go with the booking.

## "Half-Day"

Receiving a call for a "half-day" is exactly what it means. The production Coordinator only needs you for half a day (or the budget doesn't allow for a full day's expense). Though it's not ideal, it is a good way to break into a new company, anything to get your foot in the door. There are many similarities in taking a half-day booking as

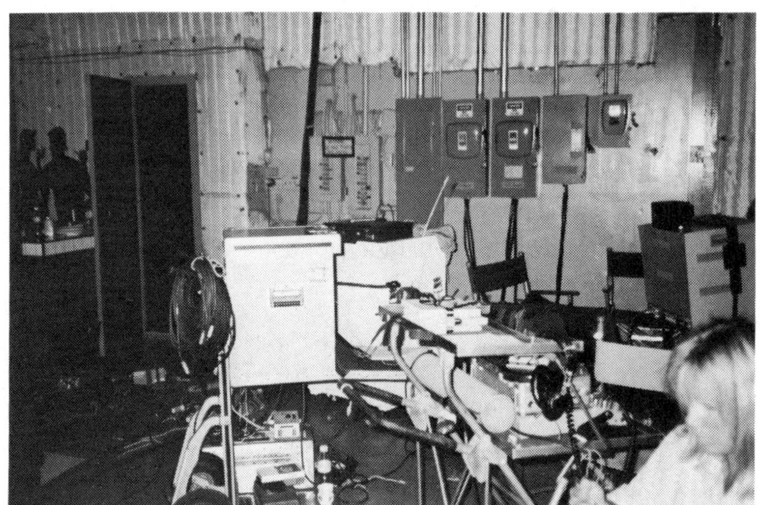

Video playback and sound equipment.  Boom person prepares for the next shot on a JACK IN THE BOX spot.

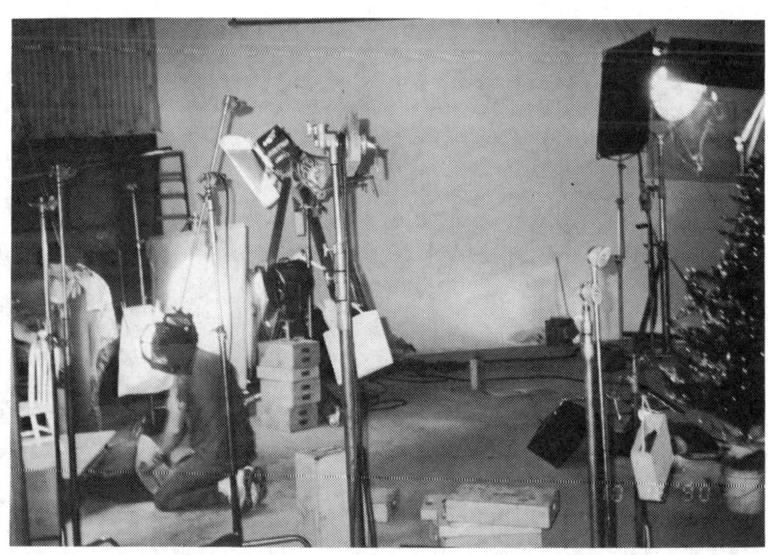

The Best Boy is tweaking the lights for the shot.

in being "On Hold". You might get a call to book a full day, week etc.; there might be a chance for a better job that comes in after you booked the half-day; etc. If you're a newcomer, chances are you won't have this problem, but after you start to work this is a serious risk. My advice is, when you start working regularly, semi-regularly, you should reconsider your career objectives and say "No" to half-days. Most Coordinators will understand.

## "Specs & Freebies"

The very last way to get your foot in the door is to work for free. Almost every film/commercial company has a new up coming Director at one time or another. This is your opportunity to get your face and talents seen by production managers, production coordinators and other crew members. Free means free no pay for the long hours that you are asked to work. They do feed you and that is a plus. It's not for everyone but it could be a way to a regular paying job. Good Luck!

On Hollywood blvd., a crew is setting up for an afternoon shot.

# CHAPTER 3

# Union Versus Nonunion Work

Early in your career in the entertainment business, you'll find yourself discussing union versus non-union work: Why is there a union? What can it do for me? Is non-union work good? There are different unions in the commercial film business, but is there a Production Assistant's union? Yes: One such union is the National Association of Broadcast Employees and Technicians (NABET) located throughout the U.S. In the union your title is described as "utility" and not Production Assistant; though the two job descriptions are identical.

Union membership is a Catch-22 situation. You cannot work for any union house until you are in the union- *but* you cannot join the union and get all the benefits until you (1) work a certain number of hours,

(2) make a certain amount of money, and (3) do so within a specified period of time. The ideal situation for resolving this is to be hired by a union company so that you can meet the union rules for the benefits. Before paying the dues/fees to join the union, make sure a union house is going to hire you on a regular basis. The union pays an hourly wage, not a flat fee (see Part 5, "Money Issues").

The other option, non-union work, offers a lot more opportunity for work but no benefits. Individuals are usually paid on a flat day-rate, and the rate is usually lower than the union rate— but not always. Remember that when you are starting out, some work is better than no work. My recommendation is, take the work when it is offered to you. You need credits and working non-union can help build your history as well as connections.

An interesting situation exists in the Union/Non-Union controversy. Even as a union member you can still work non-union jobs. The union, obviously, does not appreciate this dual standard, but thus far they have not taken an active stand on preventing members from working non-union. Maybe, they too realize that we need to work — we would rather work union but sometimes there is no other choice but to take a non-union job.

Take a lesson from the union actress who worked non-union and then took ads to announce her work. The acting union, couldn't ignore her obvious violation of their code. If you find yourself, a union member, taking non-union work, keep it to yourself.

# CHAPTER 4

## Got The Job

Attitude

Once you are hired, you must perform-not just well, but also enthusiastically. A major part of performance is attitude. A positive attitude is one of the most important things to have as a PA. This can make or break you. It is important to have a willingness to learn and lots of energy. A winning attitude is knowing that whatever is asked of you, you will do well.

Teamwork is also essential. Be flexible with your fellow workers. It is always a team effort; production is the backbone of the industry. The accolades and praise may not be apparent, but it is heart felt. Ask yourself, "How or what can I do to make the project run smoothly ?" Then do it with a smile. A smile is a must. Tell yourself, "I've been hired for a specific job and they are paying me, so I will do the best I can and always wear a *smile"*.

## Special Abilities

The Coordinator hired you because of something outstanding you said in the interview or your past performance. Be aware of the special abilities that persuaded that person to hire you. Knowing what that quality is will carry you through this job and on to the next one. Try to work closely with the Coordinator, assuring the Coordinator that you have everything under control— and make sure that you do!

## Protocol

Protocol is something you have to be aware of in business, and the film production business is no different. You are a neophyte, just starting in a business that has a history and goal of success. One common mistake is putting too much emphasis on what you think you know. Now is the time to understand that you may not have all the answers. Be helpful, make suggestions and always do your best. Be careful about trying too hard to be recognized—— especially trying to show off that you know a better way to do everything. When you take this"Know it all attitude", the negative can be, what you think you know isn't very much, and now everyone knows that you don't know anything. The system is really very simple. The Director is there to direct. The Grips and Gaffers are there to work with lighting and electrical. The Coordinator is there to coordinate pick-ups and deliveries of what is needed on the set. As a Production Assistant, you are expected to assist.  As valuable as you may think your advice may be to others, it is probably better to keep it to yourself.  Once you move up the ladder, you can do things your way, but for the time being, listen and learn, learn, learn.

There may be a time when you are asked for your opinion or ideas; this may be the time to make suggestions. Be sure your suggestions are valid.

Hertz commercial: Jeff Alves (*Center*) working as a set P.A. with O.J. Simpson, Golf great Arnold Palmer and movie and T.V. star Jamie Lee Curtis.

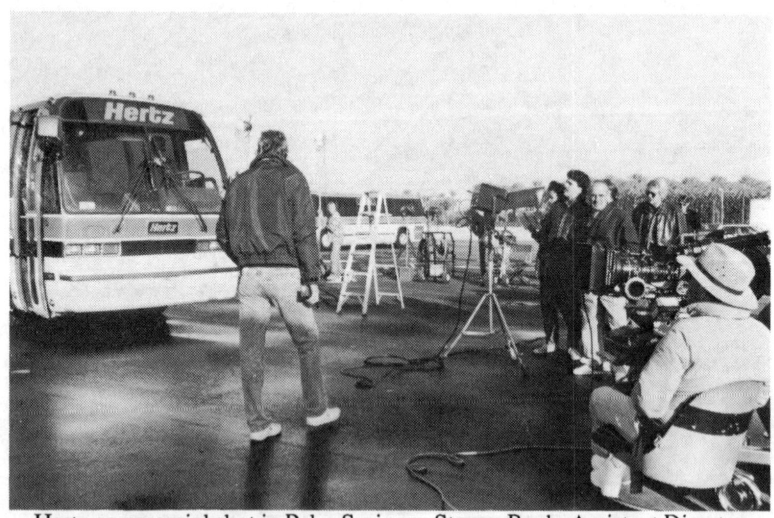

Hertz commercial shot in Palm Springs: Steven Buck, Assistant Director, (*Left*) walks back to Paul Guliner, Director, as Hertz clients check the last take to see if it was a print.

# CHAPTER 5

## Crew/Job Descriptions

PRODUCTION DEPARTMENT

Production Assistant

Production Assistant Lead

Production Coordinator

Production Manager

Unit Manager

PRODUCTION ASSISTANT LEAD

One person from whom you can learn a great deal is the production company's lead PA. As with most jobs, there is someone who has been there before you and he or she knows a little bit more than you do. Don't feel intimidated by this. Instead, use this resource to your advantage by watching and learning. Usually, a Coordinator has a PA with whom he or she has worked with for some time. The PA is hired repeatedly because the PA has done a great job for the coordinator. This experienced person is called the "Lead PA" or the "Head PA". Typically, the lead PA is working towards becoming a Coordinator. The lead is called to work first, at the start of the production, and serves as the right hand person to the coordinator. The prep include checking times and availabilities of crew members and suppliers, obtaining permits and organizing pre-pro (pre-production) meeting with clients and staff.

When the production start date gets closer, the other PAs are called in. The lead PA organizes the other PA's and makes sure that the proper things happen in the correct order. The lead has a lot of responsibility. Often, a Coordinator hires a new or green PA. It is the lead's duty to help train the new person and to guide the new person in the right ways of production. Enthusiastically learn from the guidance.

PRODUCTION ASSISTANT—DUTIES, QUALIFICATIONS, EDUCATION, WORK ENVIRONMENT, BENEFITS

A Production Assistant (PA) is the entry-level position on a film/television crew. PA's provide support and assistance to almost all areas of the production. Here are a few examples:

**Set PA:** works on the set, and may: assist security with crowd control control; escort actors to and from their trailers; deliver film to the airport or the processing lab; and help load and unload equipment. Set PA's often assist in every department, and that's a great advantage when you're getting started.

**Office PA:** works in the production office, and may perform general office work; answer phones; make copies of scripts, contracts and other documents; run errands; and assist with scheduling and shipping.

**Transportation PA:** drives a rented van, car or truck; delivers/picks up package all over town; takes actors and crew to and from the set; runs errands.

**Art Department PA:** assists with office duties; runs errands; may assist with construction of props or set dressing.

**Wardrobe PA:** assists with costumes; organizes and labels costumes; runs errands.

**Location PA:** delivers contracts; puts up signs to direct workers to the set; makes and distributes maps to locations; cleans up locations after filming; runs errands.

## Skills

Dependability—the most important skill of all.

Punctuality—absolutely essential. No excuses. If you're early, you're on time. If you're on time, you're late. If you're late, you're fired.

Ability to follow directions precisely.

Willingness to work long hours (12-14 hours days).

Professional attitude.

Knowledge of your town (directions, etc.)

Ability to "think on your feet," that is, to make a quick decision when you have to, rather than waiting helplessly for someone else take over.

Another important skill—honesty: if you make a mistake, own up to it and take responsibility.

Another important one—a thick hide. Sooner or later, you're going to get yelled at, whether or not you deserve it. Don't take it personally—get over it—everybody else does.

## Qualifications:

Previous experience is not necessary.

A dependable car is a must.

PA's do a lot of driving. If you have a good driving record, keep it that way.

Have an answering machine or pager or cell phone.

## Education:

A PA does not have to have a college degree, thought it can be helpful. Chances of being hired if you have a usable skill and a lot of enthusiasm are very good but, production companies don't hire beginners to direct or edit, they hire them as PAs.

## Work Environment:

Hours: Very, very long. Sixteen-hours days are common. You will not have any social life while you're working on a production, short or long term.

Weather: Set PAs spend most of their time out in the weather, just like the rest of the crew. So, whatever your department, dress appropriately for spending time outdoors.

Job Security: None. PA are self-employed freelancers, so real job security does not exist. Once the job is over, it's over. You depend on your good performance and professional reputation to bring the next job.

Advancement Opportunities: Great. Many, many crew members started out as PAs and moved up through the ranks. Low budget film are often the solution, offering the chance to move up the ladder to a higher position.

Benefits: Time off between jobs, whenever you wish.
Health insurance, no. It's almost never provided.
Three free meals a day, while you're working.
Great connections, good friends.
The job is never boring!
Very casual dress is the norm.

## PRODUCTION COORDINATOR

The Production Coordinator is like the second in command; this is one of the first people that the Production Manager hires. One of the first jobs of the Production Coordinator is to establish a "Home base", the actual Production Office itself. This means moving in any furniture, equipment and supplies that might be needed, as well as moving everything out once shooting is completed. This person looks after the detail work-preparing and distributing shooting schedules, crew and cast list, call sheets, production reports, as well as dispensing scripts and script revisions. Other things that have to be considered include travel arrangements, accommodations, work permits, visas, medical examinations and immunizations for crew and cast when filing in a foreign location. Finally, the Production Coordinator has to handle the paperwork and brokerage of any equipment being imported and exported; this means coordinating the pick-up and delivery of the equipment as well

## PRODUCTION MANAGER

This person works under the supervision of the producer; in fact, the Production Manager is one of the first people that the Producer hires. The Production Manager coordinates and overseas the preparation of the production unit; this means looking after off-set logistics, day to day production decisions, locations, budget schedules and personnel. The Production Manager must find and hire a crew, as well as negotiate deals for equipment rental and purchase. The Production Manager is responsible for laying the framework for the all the departments, before any official "bosses" are in place. The Production Manager must tie up loose ends at any time throughout the production process.

## UNIT MANAGER

The Unit acts as assistant to the Production Manager, and can be delegated any of the tasks listed under the Production Manager description, and then some.

## ASSISTANT DIRECTOR

Assistant Directors serve an important role in the creation of a film/

Television or a commercial. It is their job to convey every wish, every desire from the Director. Assistant Directors run the set and keep everything orderly. They let the cast and crew know when a particular shot is completed, and tell everyone what has to be set up next. The Assistant Director works closely with the Director when drafting a schedule. They must decide what is filmed, on which days, and in what order. Assistant Directors are in charge of planning and then enforcing this schedule.

## ART DEPARTMENT

Art Department types take care of everything to sets and props. They work along with the Camera Department to make sure that a film/Television or commercial looks its best. The Art Department is made up of draftsmen, painters, construction and special effects people.

## CAMERA DEPARTMENT

The Camera Department people need to know how lenses, light effects, filters, film stocks, and different types of cameras shape the way a scene looks and feels. As well, they have to know how to care for all their equipment. Most importantly, though, the Camera Department is responsible for getting a Director's creative vision on film.

## CRAFT SERVICE

The Craft Service Department often serves a dual purpose on a shoot; they supply the cast and crew with food and drink during shooting, while lending medical assistance in case of accident or injury. Healthy, interesting food can help keep the cast and crew more productive and focused.

# GRIP DEPARTMENT

The Grip Department tote grip and camera equipment around film/ Television or commercial sets for a living. The Grip Department must move and strike sets; set-up camera dollies, cranes, mounts, and platforms; and look after lights and lighting implements such as reflector boards, sandbags, c-stands. Grips also drive the trucks when transporting all there equipment from location to location.

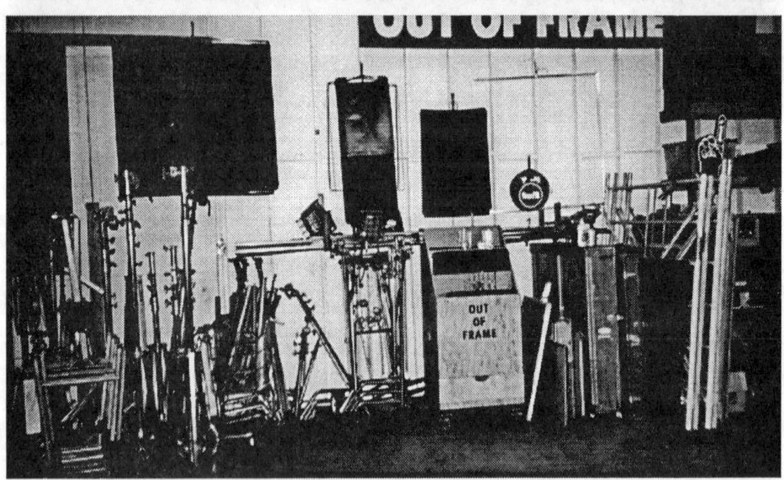


Grip equipment i.e. apple boxes, sand bags, c-stands, hi-rollers, flags, doorway dolly, traffic cones.

## SET DECORATING DEPARTMENT

The Set Decorating Department attempts to find items that are appropriate for the scene, and that fill the gap between a bare set and a natural looking location or set.

## LIGHTING/ELECTRICS DEPARTMENT

This Department is responsible for illuminating performers, sets, and on screen action in general. Lighting is important to any film/television or commercial. In the end, the Director of Photography gets the final say as to what role lighting plays; but other people with input on the decision include the Director and the Production Designer.

## PROPS DEPARTMENT

The Props Department supplies and looks after any props that may be required for a film/television or commercial. One of the first duties of the Props Department is to break down the script scene by scene and decide which articles are required. The Props Department then tries to make or find props that fit in with what the scene requires, while at the same time conforming to the Director's overall creative vision. Once all the props are ready to go, this Department makes sure that they make it to the set on the right day.

## LOCATION DEPARTMENT

The Locations Department is responsible for finding viable venues where shooting can take place. A location might include outdoor areas, existing buildings, or places that can be easily accommodate a set. The Locations Department is one of the first Departments to be hired and is one of the last to stop working.

© Spyglass Entertainment Group, LP. (Right) Writer/ Director M. Night Shyamalan and the director of photography Tak Fujimoto, A.S.C. prepare to shoot a scene for THE SIXTH SENSE.

(Below) M. Night Shyamalan and Bruce Willis discuss an upcoming scene. *Photo courtesy of Ron Phillips.*

# PART TWO
## ~Shooting~

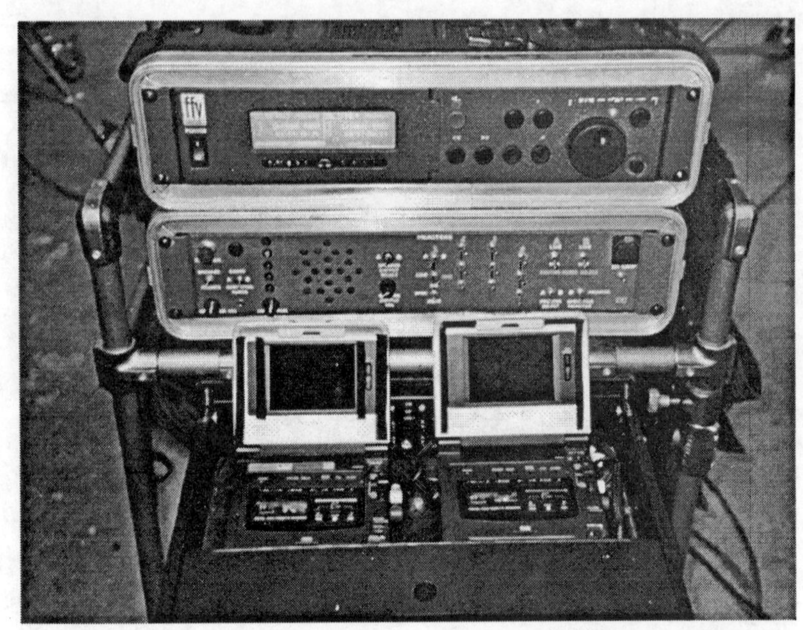

(Above) Video assist package, front view.  Operated by a VTR crew person.

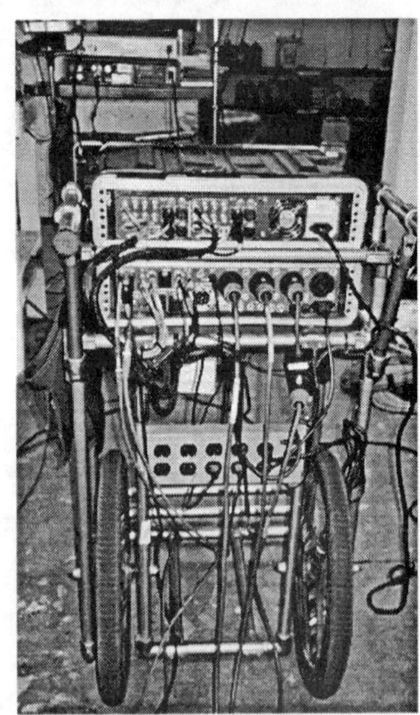

(Right)  Back view of the video assist package.

# CHAPTER 6

## The Production Cycle

Knowing how a film production runs its cycle is very important. To help understand the process, I'll describe a one-day shoot (that is, one day of filming) commercial cycle. The procedure for films is very similar, but the entire cycle can span up to a year or more. The time frame for commercials is much more condensed.

### Prep Day

On the *prep* day, the Coordinator and the Producer prepare for the commercial's *shoot* day. Preparation entails the Coordinator communicating with the Clients, the Agency, and the Director, discussing every detail of the commercial (making phone calls, and meeting face to face with all parties). This day requires a lot of running

around, and it can be very frustrating.  Nonetheless, keep smiling:
You're still learning.  The key is to learn as much as possible, as
quickly as possible.

## Shoot Day

The *shoot* day is why you are all there.  It's usually an early day.
Energy runs high on this day.  As a PA, you will get to the stage or
location before any other crew members.  Here is a little tip: If you are
<u>on time</u>, you are <u>15 minutes late</u>.  The performance of a PA on this day
is a "trial" by the people in charge, and you should be aware of this.

## Wrap Day

The *wrap* day is the day on which everything that was used is to be
returned in good condition and on time.  Also, this is a day on which
all the loose ends get tied up.  The chapters that follow will go into
more detail about the prep, wrap, and shoot days.  Though each aspect
of the production cycle is essential, the central feature of your job is
to ensure that everything goes well during the shoot.  The preparation
and wrap-up tasks are described fully in "Part 4 : Other Duties."

# CHAPTER
# 7

## The Shot:
## The Most Important Thing

Being a PA entails multitudinous detail, from the start to the finish of production, in the office, at the shoot, and in the wrap. Nonetheless, anyone in the business will say that getting the "shot" is most important of all, even though you and many others spend long hours prepping for and wrapping after the shoot. The Camera Operator and the Director (in some cases, this is the same person) have been compiling all their ideas and are waiting to catch that magical moment on film.

Once shooting is ready to begin, the Assistant Director "AD" becomes your boss on the set. The Coordinator is the person who hired you and is your main boss, but you are there now to help everybody.

Sometimes you might feel that you have 4 or 5 bosses, that is not unusual. The AD is hired to get the shot completed on time, so if he or she needs help, it is your job to help. The AD, and the Coordinator know the best priorities for your time and effort. Go with the flow, and make sure you're wearing a smile. You are paid to be helpful.

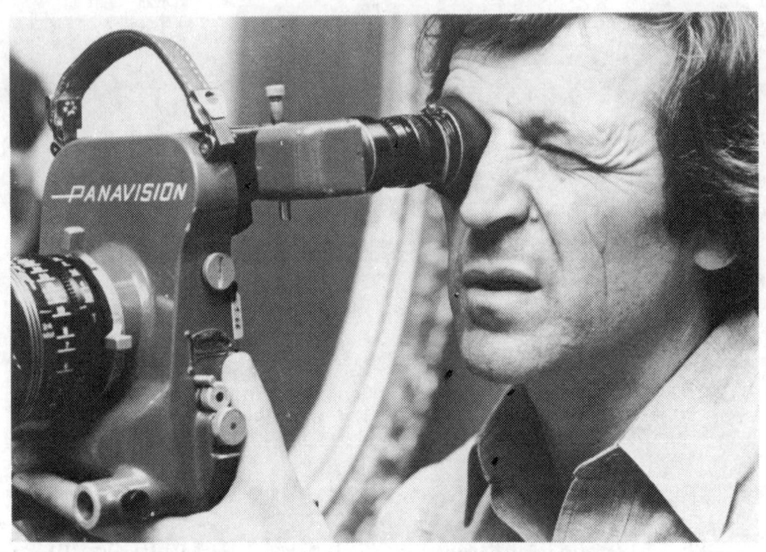

Director Costa-Gavras checks a shot for "MISSING." *Courtesy of Universal Pictures/Polygram Pictures Presentation.*

# CHAPTER 8

## Handling The Film
## Moviola
## Dailies Package

Delivering the Dailies

*Dailies* refer to the film that has been shot and is being developed at the lab, to be screened the next day. For example, at the end of the shoot day, the Assistant cameraman downloads (removes for processing) the magazines (containers) of film. The Coordinator gives a *purchase order* (PO) to the Assistant Cameraman or the Second Assistant Cameraman to be filled out and attached to the cans going to the lab for processing.

The PA will receive the cans of film from the camera department to be dropped off at the lab (customer service is where the film is usually received). The lab takes 6 to 12 hours to develop the film. The next day, you will return to the lab to pick up the finished product and get it ready for screening in a screening room or on a moviola or on a dallies package (3/4" deck with a large monitor for viewing) see page 43.

## Racking up the Moviola  (Old Method)

Learning to rack up the dailies onto the moviola can and will increase your pay rate. The philosophy here is that the more you know, the more you will be worth. Many times, you will be asked whether you know how to rack up a moviola. This takes practice to learn how to do well.

Pressures come with this job. The dailies are what everybody, including the Director, the Producer, the Coordinator, the Clients, and the Agency are waiting for. Don't sweat it. take your time, do it right, and make sure that all the speeds are set on "slow" to start. Make sure the loops are large enough not to tear the film.

If you don't know how to rack up the moviola, learn. Find someone who will show you, preferably on your own time. Then when the question comes up, you can say, yes!

## Avoiding Hassles

Unless you specify otherwise, the film might come from the lab upside-down, "tails out" (i.e., backwards) and sometimes in ways you didn't think film could be placed on a spool. To avoid these problems, ask the Assistant Cameraman to write on the purchase order going to the lab, "Heads Out."

This means that the lab will, 99% of the time, rewind the film so it is side up on the reel. If they do so you can quickly and easily rack it onto the moviola without having to rewind it yourself. Rewinding is a hassle and a waste of time, let the lab do it. The proper term for correctly rewound film is "the emulsion-side up, and heads out". When racking up the moviola, the black line on the film goes closest to the moviola.

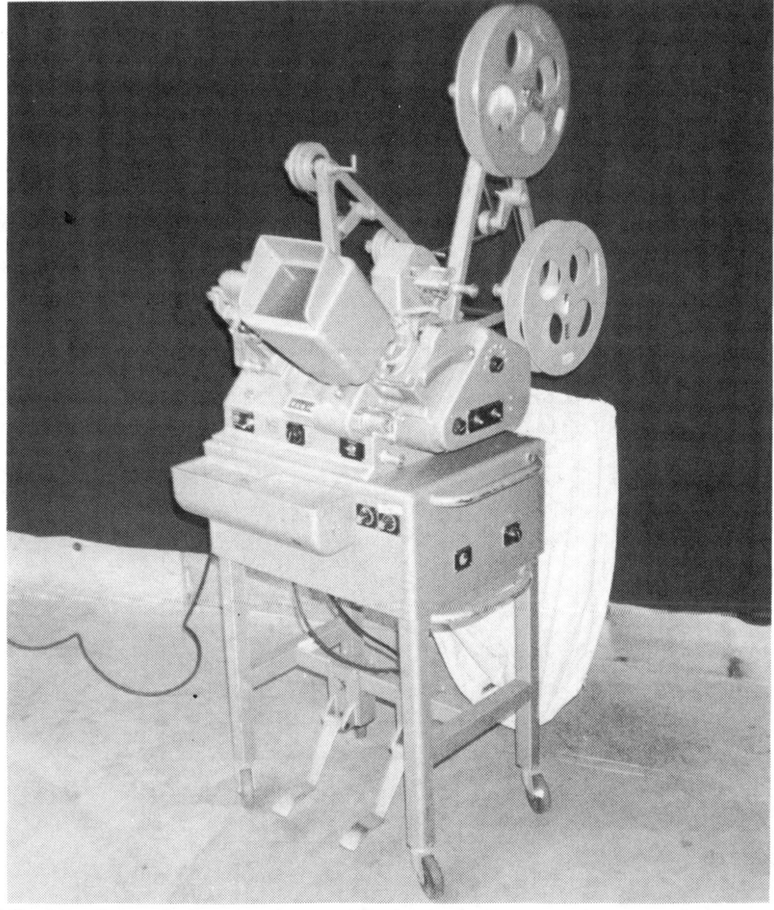

The film that was shot that day or night is viewed by this machine. This is one of the older methods, today they use simpler methods i.e. VHS, CD or DVD.

Following are specific instructions and diagrams to show you *exactly* how to rack up a moviola, the information was provided by Hal Dennis Productions, Hollywood, CA.

# PREPARATION FOR USE
## 35 MM

## IMPORTANT:

1. Check for adequate loop sizes between lower feed sprocket and gate, and between intermittent sprocket and upper feed sprocket. Film loop size must be large enough to prevent film tension but small enough to prevent film rubbing against machine.

2. Turn flywheel by hand to check movement of film and film loops.

3. Remove slack between jerk absorber rollers and reels.

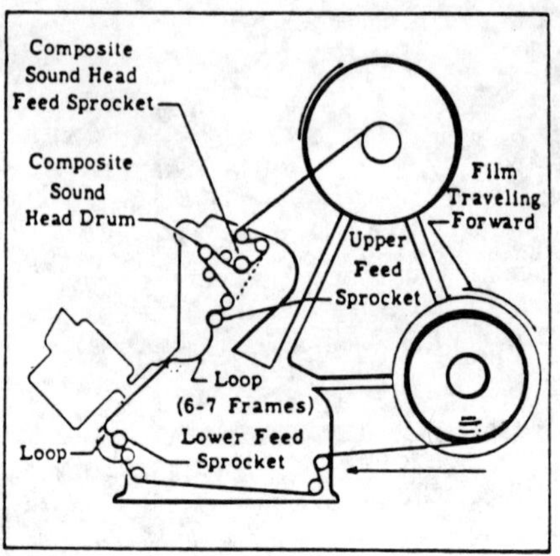


Figure 1.  Film Threading, 35mm Machine

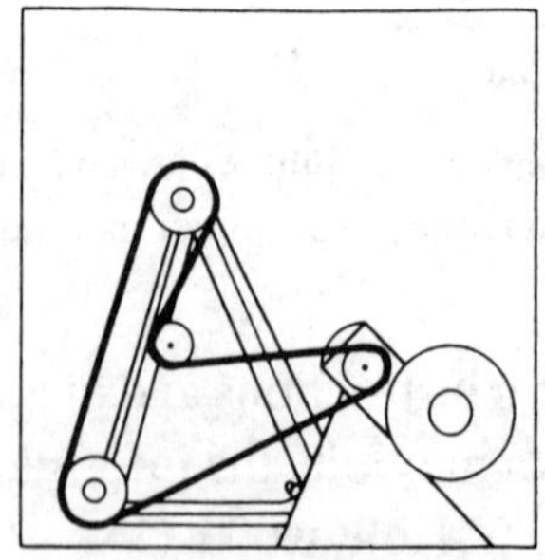

Figure 2.  Belt Placement

<u>Single Sound Head Machine</u>

The center volume control knob on the main body is the sound volume control. An amplifier OFF switch is integral with the VOLUME CONTROL.

<u>Double Sound Head Machines</u>

On machines incorporating two sound heads, the center VOLUME CONTROL knob controls the volume as for a single sound head; in addition, each EXCITER LAMP reheostat controls exciter lamp intensity of the nearest head giving independent control of each sound head.

IMPORTANT: If only one optical sound head is in use, or if the magnetic sound is in use, be certain that the EXCITER LAMP rheostats for non-operating optical sound units are in the off position.

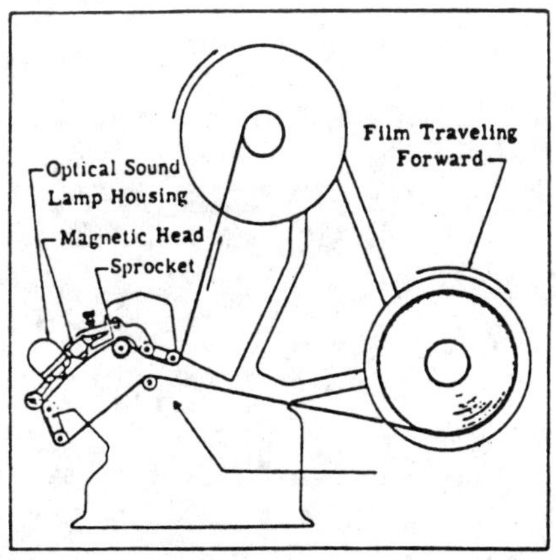


Figure 3. Separate Sound Head Film Threading Diagram

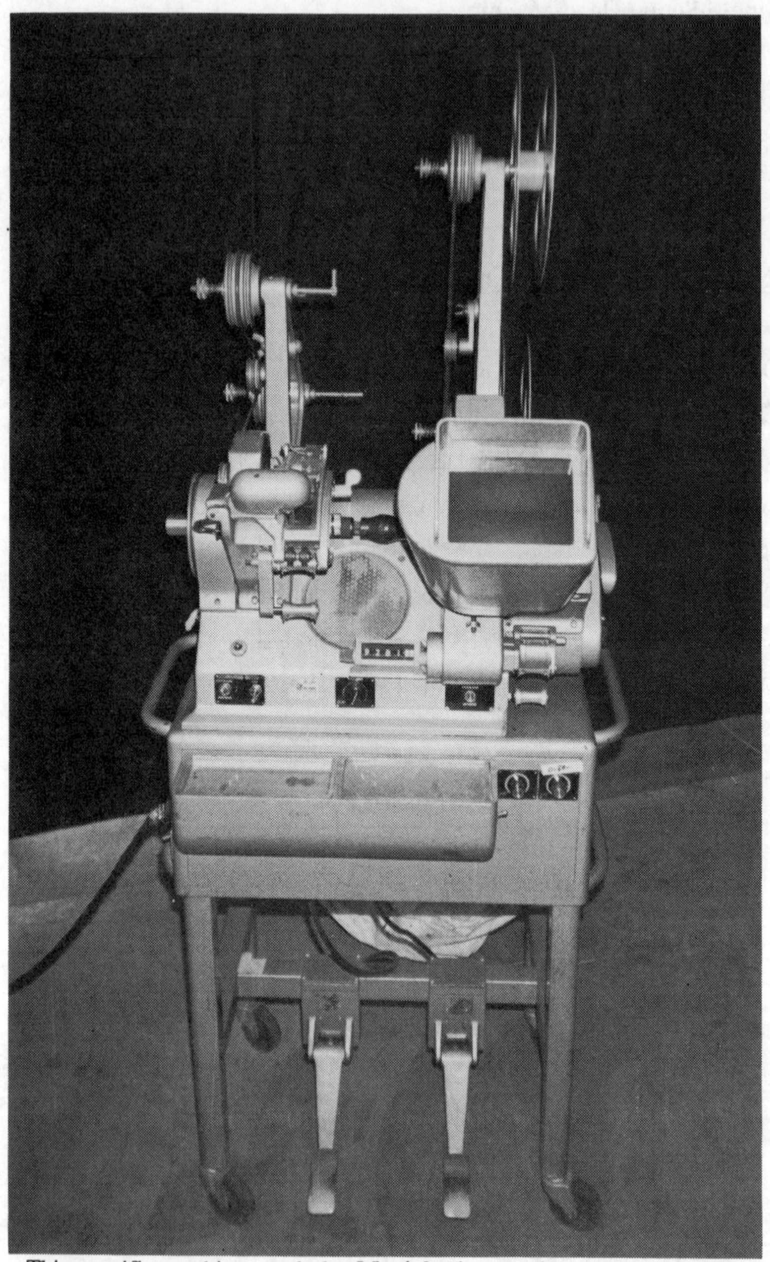

This specific machine, made by **Moviola**, is run by a motor and is generally equipped to handle a single reel of motion picture film and a single sound track.

## Dailies Package

The dailies package consists of a 3/4" plackback deck and usually a 17" to 24" monitor (cable, input and outputs, ready). At the time of wrap of the film or commercial, the Production Manager or Coordinator will decide which way the director wants to view his developed film and  write on the camera report for the processing lab the method or any special instructions. When you go back to the processing lab you will know if you're getting the processed film on 3/4" tape or on the standard reel. This information is very helpful, the following day.

Pictured are a 3/4" video deck and a 24" monitor used on set to view the film or video, shot that day or night.

© Lam Ping Ltd. (Top) Producer/Director Peter Weir on location to shoot a scene for the romantic comedy GREEN CARD. (Bottom) Peter Weir (left) and his stars Andie MacDowell (center) and Gérard Depardieu (right) rehearse a scene for the film. *Photo courtesy of Francois Duhamel.*

# Part Three
## ~Tools of the Trade~

24/7 Expendable Store carries a wide variety of expendables and is becoming one of the major expendable stores in Hollywood.

Pictured are production bags from our friends at *Cinebags and Setwear*. These are the most widely used in the film industry.

# CHAPTER 9

## Equipment Bag

To do the best job possible it is imperative you have the right tools. You can usually keep your equipment in a lightweight carrying case or bag. Your equipment bag should have the following features:

1. Shoulder straps, or at least handles.

2. Easy access for opening, closing, storing, and removing equipment.

3. Lightweight but sturdy design; able to take a beating (canvas and nylon provide this characteristic, a briefcase is impractical for this reason).

4. Many compartments in which to hold several items separately.

As you read the list of suggested equipment, you will see why I suggest the above features for your equipment bag.

The reason to have equipment is to make your job easier and more efficient. Don't rush out and spend a lot of money that you don't have for the first job. You should, however, gradually pick up more equipment. When I first started, all I had was a piece of paper in my back pocket and a pen in my front pocket, to note names, time, and places to pick up gear. A complete equipment bag will develop over a period of time. The more equipment you have to do your job effectively, the easier it will be.

Also, you should know how to set-up and break down a directors chair and know how to use a screw gun. These my seem like simple tasks at first, but, it does take practice. You want your employer to feel confident that this is not your first job. It is easy to call up a rental house and ask if you can come in and practice.

Here are a few things you should have in your bag:

| | |
|---|---|
| 1* Local Street guide | 2. Writing implements |
| 3. Padlock with key | 4. Matte knife |
| 5. Self stick notes | 6. Belt |
| 7. Pocket calculator | 8. Felt tip markers |
| 9. **Production Directories | 10. Note pad |
| 11. Bottle opener | 12. Mini stapler |
| 13. Buck knife | 14. Invoice book |
| 15. Mini mag light | 16. Source book |
| 17. Cell phone | 18. Pager |
| 19. Gloves/clip | 20. Laptop |

* In Los Angeles the Thomas Brothers Guide
* www.mapquest.com


**LA411 Los Angeles Directory
**NY411 New York Directory
**The Reel Directory San Francisco Directory
**The Creative Industry Handbook Los Angeles Directory
**The Not For Tourist Guide

# CHAPTER 10

## Paperwork

Call Sheet

It is a necessity for all PAs to know both what a *call sheet* is and how to read one. A call sheet consists of (1) the crew and their job titles (2) equipment suppliers and their phone number (3) job name and number (4) day and time (5) location of the shoot (6) Talent, etc. (See the sample "Call Sheet" at the end of this chapter).

Production Report

A *production report* is a report of the day-by-day production activities. It includes: (1) when the crew starts (2) when the talent arrives (3) the equipment used (4) type of film used, etc. It is as important as a call sheet and is usually filled out throughout the day. If there is a First AD or a Second AD, this is his or her duty;  if not, the Coordinator fills it out. Try to learn how to fill this out; anything that you can learn to help a Coordinator makes you more valuable as a PA (See the sample "Daily Production Report"  form at the end of this chapter).

# CALLSHEET

DATE:_________________

CALLTIME:____ JOB NO: ____

LOCATION__________ STAGE:______ AT:_________________

_______________________ PHONE:______ PRODUCT:__________

CLIENTS __________ HOTEL:______ AGENCY:__________

_______________________ PHONE:______ DAY:________ OF:______

MOS  SYNC  TAPE  16MM  35MM
☐    ☐     ☐     ☐      ☐

| Category | Name Phone # | Time IN | Time Out | Category | Name Phone # | Time IN | Time Out |
|---|---|---|---|---|---|---|---|
| DIRECTOR | | | | GAFFER | | | |
| PRODUCER | | | | BEST BOY | | | |
| DIR.PHOTO. | | | | ELEC. | | | |
| PROD. MGR. | | | | ELEC. | | | |
| CAMERA | | | | KEY | | | |
| ASST.CAM. | | | | GRIP | | | |
| ASST. DIR. | | | | GRIP | | | |
| STYLIST | | | | PROPS. | | | |
| MAKE-UP | | | | PROPS. | | | |
| MIXER | | | | PA | | | |
| BOOM | | | | PA | | | |
| VTR | | | | PA | | | |

| TALENT: NAME AND # | AGENCY & PHONE NO. | CALL TIME | SPOTS |
|---|---|---|---|
| 1._____________ | | | |
| 2._____________ | | | |
| 3._____________ | | | |
| 4._____________ | | | |
| 5._____________ | | | |
| 6._____________ | | | |

# *CallSheet*

JOB#

AGENCY:
AGENCY PRODUCER:

LOCATION:

SHOOT DAY:

NAME          PHONE#

EXEC. PRODUCER:
PRODUCER:
DIRECTOR:
DIRECTOR OF PHOTOGRAPHY:
ASST. CAMERA:
ASST. DIRECTOR:
GAFFER:
BEST BOY:
ELEC.
KEY GRIP:
GRIP:
GRIP TRUCK DRIVER:
STUDIO TEACHER:
PROP. MASTER:
SET. DRESSER:
SCRIPT:
SOUND:
MAKE-UP:
VTR:
WARDROBE:
PRODUCTION ASST.
PRODUCTION ASST.
PRODUCTION ASST.
CRAFT SERVICE:

# DAILY PRODUCTION REPORT

| ADVERTISING AGENCY: | | PRODUCT AND TITLE: | DATE: | M T W T F S S |
|---|---|---|---|---|

| PRODUCTION # | LAB. FILM | STOCK | LAB.SOUND | LOCATIONS |
|---|---|---|---|---|
| | | FOOTAGE EXPOSED TO DATE: | | |
| TRUCK CALL | | | | |
| CREW CALL | | FOOTAGE EXPOSED | | |
| 1ST SHOT | | | | |
| LUNCH START | | | | |
| LUNCH END | | | | |
| 1ST PM SHOT | | WEATHER: | | |
| SUPPER START | | | | |
| SUPPER END | | | | |
| WRAP CAMERA | | | | |
| CREW WRAP | | | | |

## EQIUPMENT

CAMERA:

GENERATOR:

SOUND:

ELECTRICAL:

GRIP:

DOLLY:

WALKIE-TALKIE

TRANSPORTATION:

CATERING:

REMARKS:

# DAILY PRODUCTION REPORT

## (REAR)

PRODUCT:                                            JOB NO.

DAY-DATE:                                      PRODUCER:

| CATEGORY | NAME | IN | L | D | OUT | CATEGORY | NAME | IN | L | D | OUT |
|---|---|---|---|---|---|---|---|---|---|---|---|
| DIRECTOR |  |  |  |  |  | GAFFER |  |  |  |  |  |
| ASST. DIR |  |  |  |  |  | BEST BOY |  |  |  |  |  |
| COORD. |  |  |  |  |  | ELEC. |  |  |  |  |  |
| CAMERA |  |  |  |  |  | KEY GRIP |  |  |  |  |  |
| SCRIPT |  |  |  |  |  | GRIP |  |  |  |  |  |
| MAKE-UP |  |  |  |  |  | SFX |  |  |  |  |  |
| HAIR |  |  |  |  |  | PROPS. |  |  |  |  |  |
| MIXER |  |  |  |  |  | PA |  |  |  |  |  |
| VTR |  |  |  |  |  | PA |  |  |  |  |  |
| STYLIST |  |  |  |  |  | PA |  |  |  |  |  |
|  |  |  |  |  |  |  |  |  |  |  |  |

## TALENT

| NAME | TELEPHONE | CATEGORY | IN | LUNCH | DINNER | OUT |
|---|---|---|---|---|---|---|
|  |  |  |  |  |  |  |
|  |  |  |  |  |  |  |
|  |  |  |  |  |  |  |
|  |  |  |  |  |  |  |
|  |  |  |  |  |  |  |
|  |  |  |  |  |  |  |
|  |  |  |  |  |  |  |
|  |  |  |  |  |  |  |

# CHAPTER 11

## Walkie-Talkies
## Cellular Phones
## Pagers
## Gear Labels

Walkie-talkies are used to communicate with persons who can't be by your side all the time. They are used to ensure everybody involved in the production is on the same wave length. Everyone must be completely aware of what place and what changes might have to be made in order for the production to run smoothly. The best example of the need for effective communication is location shooting, when the crew might be separated by one or more physical miles. If so, the walkie-talkie may be your only form of communication with others involved in the shoot.

Walkie-talkies run on removable batteries, located either on the bottom or the side of the unit. They differ in size, range, type, and style and some are adaptable to headsets. Mountains or downtown buildings might limit units' range or lower or even cut off the units' ability to respond. Physical obstructions might also hinder communication.

Walkie-talkies offer a valuable means of communication. Be aware that when engaging in conversation you must be direct and to the point with questions and answers; speak clearly and don't mumble. Remember, what you say can be heard by everyone.

Before handing out the walkie-talkies be sure all antennas are attached, they are turned on and that they are set on the same channel, usually channel 1.

Keep a record of who gets each unit. Sometimes they disappear and it can be useful knowing who had had it last. A good idea is to number each unit by adding a Gear Label; then log each unit in and out.

Cellular phones have become a valued communication asset in the film industry, from the Director, Producer, Production manager and Coordinator and Production Assistants. If you own your cellular phone it is the best way to go. Production companies rent cellular phones for the duration of the film or commercial.

Also, pager and especially two-way pagers have been a communication asset. Although it is only number or text messaging that keeps you in touch with the Production Manager or Coordinator, it is better than nothing.

Gear Labels are a new way of labeling walkie-talkies for the film or commercial. It saves time, just peel off the label, apply and write on the crews name.

Next is a variety of terms that you will hear consistently, with limited variations on most sets.

# WALKIE-TALKIE LINGO

| | |
|---|---|
| Copy? or Did you copy? | —Do you hear me, clearly? |
| 10/4 | —A positive response |
| Copy that | —Did you hear me? |
| Roger that | —Understand |
| What's your 20 | —Where are you? |
| Go to 2 | —Switch to channel 2 on the walkie-talkie |
| Back to 1 | —Switch back to channel 1 |
| Hold Traffic | —Don't let cars or people through |
| Release Traffic | —Let the cars and people through. |
| Watch your back | —Get out of the way |
| Flashing | —Used before an insta-matic camera that has a flash attached. ( Never fire a flash when film or tape is rolling). |

The walkie-talkies pictures on the following pages were supplied to us by White Castle Communication Rentals.

The 1225 model is widely used by the film and Television industry.

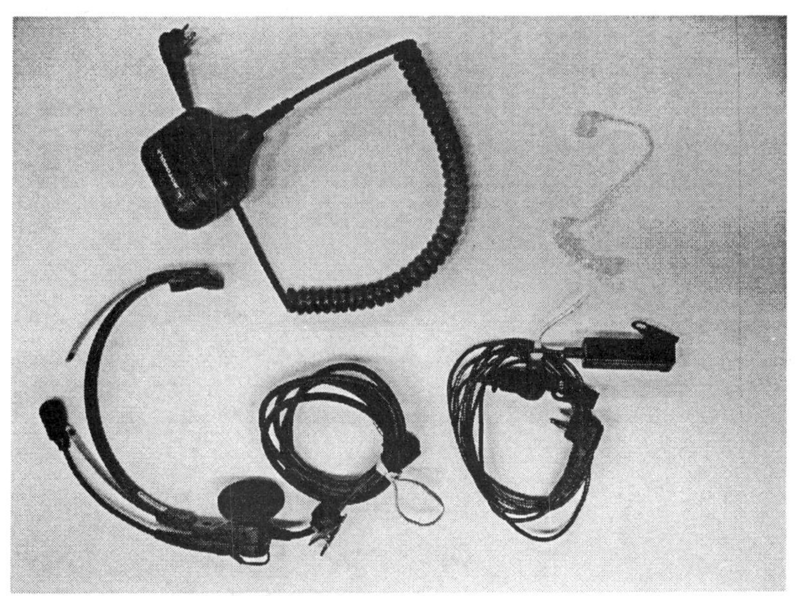

Pictured are a Motorola lightweight headset, Motorola hand mic and an Otto surveillance headset.

Pictured is a Samsung cell phone with accessories.

Gear Labels
www.gearlabels.com

# PART FOUR
## ~Duties of a Production Assistant~

A production lighting package stored on stage.

The Grips area:  C-stands, apple boxes, wedges, sandbags, etc.

# CHAPTER 12

## Obtaining Equipment and Supplies

Your role during the shoot is important, but perhaps even more important to the team effort is your role in preparing for the shoot. It is your job to see to it that all the equipment and supply needs of everybody on the production team are met. It can be quite a daunting task to attend to every last detail of a production site. If you can do this well, you've proven yourself indispensable to the team.

Most of the rental equipment has to be picked up prior to the beginning of the shoot and dropped off at the end. Some supplies and specialized items, however, must be picked up daily. Do this aspect of your job willingly, pleasantly, and efficiently, and your efforts will be appreciated.

Though you do have to pick up and deliver all the equipment and supplies, you aren't required to order them. The Coordinator calls the vendors (suppliers of equipment or materials) to request the equipment. When the Coordinator orders the materials, he or she tells the supplier the specific (purchase order) number so that no two orders have the same PO number, and each purchase can be tracked individually according to the PO number.

The following are the key tasks of a PA in regard to equipment and supplies:

1. Get the POs for all the gear to be picked up in one trip (usually from the Coordinator or from accounting personnel)

2. Check out the van or truck in which the equipment is to be picked up. Make sure that you have rope and furniture pads and any other materials you might need for securely storing the gear. Don't forget gas, oil and water to keep the vehicle running.

3. Plan a route for picking up the gear (knowing the locations of vendors and the stage in the area will make your job easier). Remember the *Local Street Guide* from Chapter 9.

4. Go to each vendor, present the PO to the vendor, and wait for the vendor to gather the requested items.

5. Before leaving with the items(s), confirm that each item on the PO was received and that the condition of each item was satisfactory(you're responsible for this and for returning each item in the same condition in which it was received). Assuming that all is satisfactory, you will sign a form confirming that you received the equipment in good condition.

6. Loading can be an easy task if you just stop and get organized. You have already picked up the rental vehicle, truck or van. The standard is a cube enclosed truck, anywhere between 14ft. to 24 ft.

Production Equipment truck, interior.

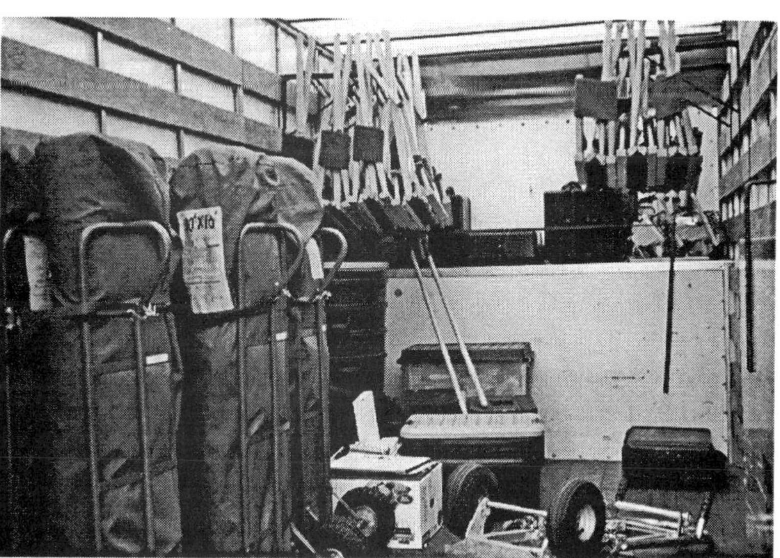

Close-up of the interior.

or 26ft long. This vehicle should have a boxed or opened back. Securely store the goods in the van or truck, using the rope and furniture pads as needed.

7. Proceed with steps 4 through 6 until all items are retrieved.

8. If the items aren't to be delivered to the shoot location at this time, make sure that they are stored securely until the time of delivery (e.g., not leaving the film sitting in sunlight or exposing sensitive equipment to extreme temperatures). If storage is not needed, proceed directly to Step 9.

9. Deliver the items to the production site, making sure that each item is placed exactly where it is needed. Generally, you should unload the camera gear first, then the other items that must be used right away, then items that aren't needed until later. If you plan your pick-up route unloading will be a cinch.

10. Once the camera gear is under the watchful eye of the First Assistant Camera Operator, it's time to prepare to feed the crew.

**NOTE:** Propmtness pays. Be on time when you are picking up or delivering items. Learning to do all aspects of your job (even the tedious ones) with a positive attitude will advance your career and make you far more marketable for future work. To truly excel as a PA, you should be pleasant and efficient and so unobtrusive that things seem magically to appear on time and in place—out of no-where.

# CHAPTER 13

## Feeding The Crew

In addition to delivering the production equipment and supplies, you are responsible for another crucial supply for the crew: food and beverages. You must ensure that the crew eats well and enjoyably. Never undervalue this crucial service to the crew. Having adequate beverages and foods available can calm irritated tempers, smooth rough edges, and make everyone on the crew more productive.

The term used for this food and beverage service is *craft service*. Several items are essential to good craft service:

1. One or two tables (or more, depending on the size of the crew and of the tables).

2.  At least two coolers:  one for soft drinks and one for water. Also check to see if you have access to running water.  Water  is a ***must*** if you  manage never to run out of water,  you'll have many allies on the set.  If you don't have running water, always fill both coolers with ice first thing in the morning. Through the day, double check and refill your water supply if need be.

3.  A coffee urn (full of fresh, hot coffee) and a complete supply of cups, cream, sugar, artificial sweetener, and stirrers.

4.  A hot-water urn and an assortment of alternatives to coffee (e.g., tea and other beverages for those who don't drink coffee). Double check not to fill a coffee urn with hot water. Always keep the hot water urn separate.  Tea and soup drinkers don't like their beverage to taste like coffee.

5.  An appropriate selection of foodstuff,  depending on the budget, the number of the crew members and so on.

6.  Keep the area clean. Put out plenty of garbage bags.  The crew should not have to search for a place to throw trash.

On shoot days, the production company hires a caterer, whom you help in setting up for the crew's breakfast.  After 3-4 hours, put away the breakfast food, and bring out some snacks for munching ( cheese, crakers and fruit) until it's time for lunch.  After lunch the crew usually has a sweet tooth, candy and cookies.  As dinner draws near try chips, dips and specialty items— anything you have left in your food hoard.

**TIPS:**

1. *Never* run out of water.

2. Avoid running out of food or beverages —— restock the soda coolers and replenish food trays frequently.

3. Frequently clean up around the food area, tossing out gargage, wiping spills, and otherwise making the food area appealing.

4. *Never* begin eating before the other crew members have had the chance to eat. This pratice you must accept until you have advanced and are no longer a PA.

5. Try to find out in advance how many members of the crew will be present each day, and estimate your food purchases accordingly.

Unlike the production equipment and supplies, the purchases of foodstuff will be made from petty cash, which is discussed fully in the next Chapter.

Examples of craft service foods:

| | |
|---|---|
| Cheese | Ice |
| Crackers | Licorice |
| Gum | Sodas (diet & reg.) |
| Potato Chips | Paper Plates |
| Fruit | Plastics Untensils |
| Vegetables | Paper Cups |
| Cookies | Trash Bags |
| Beef Jerky | Paper Towels |
| Bag Candy | Toilet Paper |
| Water | Popcorn |

(Get special requests from the Coordinator.)

During the filming of a movie, feeding the crew on the Universal Studios back lot is a daunting task.

In Hollywood, Calif., a catering truck getting ready to serve the crew.

# CHAPTER 14

## Petty Cash

As mentioned in Chapter 13, not all expenses are paid via POs (purchase orders). Foodstuffs (other than those supplied by caterers) and some props, wardrobe, hardware, rentals, fees, and other items are paid for out of "petty cash". *Petty cash* is money given to a PA by a Coordinator; the PA uses it to cover expenses incurred for completion of the job. It is money that has been budgeted for production expenses; such expenses are usually less expensive than the items purchased with a PO.

At the start of production, the Coordinator will sign out a specific amount of money for you to monitor and use as petty cash for production expenses. To underscore your responsibility for this money, the Coordinator will ask you to count the money and sign a receipt confirming the amount given to you . The amount on the receipt (called a "chit") is the amount for which you will be responsible until the end of production. At the end of production, you must return to the Coordinator exactly the same amount, either in cash receipts for purchases or in cash left over after all purchases were made. If you do not have a cash receipt for an item, you will be expected to make up the difference "out of pocket". The need for a receipt for each purchase is obvious.

Three things make it easier to track the petty cash (PC):

1. When you first receive the petty cash, put the money into a *petty cash* envelope. Be sure to note the name of the job and the job number along with your name and phone number on the envelope. Usually PC envelopes are supplied by the production company. Use that envelope for all your receipts, as well as for the cash.

2. As you acquire receipts number them in chronological order. Try to keep your numbering in the same location on the receipts, etc. lower right or upper right seem to be favored. After each receipt is numbered it will be recorded next to the corresponding number on the "Summary of job Advance Disbursements" which is the PC envelope.

3. On the PC envelope, neatly and carefully record each expenditure, noting the date, amount, category of expense, and brief explanation of the expense. It is best to use a pencil, especially if you are prone to simple numerical errors. A sample of the form is included at the end of this chapter.

**NOTE:** On the form, you'll notice a place to indicate "Balance Due Employee." On occasion, you may have to purchase items out of your own pocket and seek reimbursement from the production company. Avoid this if at all possible because it is not only a problem for you but also a problem for whoever figured the budget based on a smaller amount of expenses from petty cash.

Any time that you are responsible for petty cash, guard it carefully, and document each expenditure.  You will go broke quickly if you have to make frequent cash compensations for items you purchased without getting receipts. Before you turn in your completed envelope and disbursements, make a copy of the expenditures for your records.

AMOUNT $_________________          NO._____________

### RECEIVED OF PETTY CASH

_________ 20______

FOR_______________________________________________

CHARGE TO_________________________________________

APPROVED BY                    RECEIVED BY

_______________                _______________

Petty cash (PC) chit.

AMOUNT $____________          NO.___________

### RECEIVED OF PETTY CASH

_________________20________

FOR_______________________________________________________

CHARGE TO_________________________________________________

_________________________________________________________

APPROVED BY                    RECEIVED BY

______________________        ______________________________

---

AMOUNT $______________

### RECEIVED OF PETTY CASH

_____________20_________

FOR_______________________________________________________

CHARGE TO_________________________________________________

_________________________________________________________

__________________                    ________________

APPROVED BY                                    RECEIVED BY

PETTY CASH

Use Separate Envelope for
Each Job Number

JOB NAME___________  JOB#________  PAGE NO. ______

EMPLOYEE__________________

| EXPLANATION | DATE | AMOUNT | PROPS | TOLLS | MEALS | CAR | LUNCH | DINNER |
|---|---|---|---|---|---|---|---|---|
| 1 | | | | | | | | |
| 2 | | | | | | | | |
| 3 | | | | | | | | |
| 4 | | | | | | | | |
| 5 | | | | | | | | |
| 6 | | | | | | | | |
| 7 | | | | | | | | |
| 8 | | | | | | | | |
| 9 | | | | | | | | |
| 10 | | | | | | | | |
| 11 | | | | | | | | |
| 12 | | | | | | | | |
| 13 | | | | | | | | |
| 14 | | | | | | | | |
| 15 | | | | | | | | |

| TOTAL DISBURSED | |
|---|---|
| AMOUNT RECEIVED | |
| BAL. DUE EMPLOYEE | |
| BAL. DUE CO. | |

SIGNATURE OF EMPLOYEE ______________________________

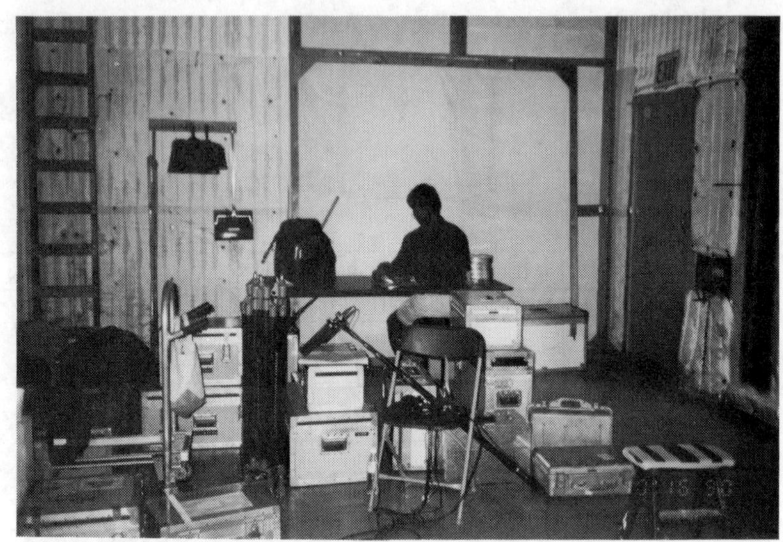

The Assistant Cameraman, down loading film, on an Emporium Capwell
commercial produced by Levinson, Israelson & Bell Production Company.

Set of a Christmas commercial.

# CHAPTER 15

## It's A Wrap

Recall from Chapter 6 that a wrap signifies that on-site production of the movie, film, or television program is complete. It does not, however, mean that your job has ended. Chapter 12 mentioned all the duties needed for preparing for the shoot. Once shooting has ended, all those tasks must be done in reverse:

1. Get (or make) a list of all the items that must be returned (check the POs, as needed).

2. At the production site, gather up all the items to be returned, check their condition (reporting to the Coordinator any potential problems), and make sure that all the items are stored securely in the van or truck, using the rope and furniture pads (as needed) until the time of return.

3. Plan your route of returning the gear (modify your original route, as needed).

4. Go to each vendor, showing the equipment, and waiting for the vendor to confirm the condition of the returned items.

5. Return the van or truck to the production company, and clean it out thoroughly, returning ropes and furniture pads or other materials.

6. Once the van or truck has been cleaned, deliver it to the rental agency.

**NOTE:** Any time you are dealing with rented property of any kind, make sure that it is in at least as good a condition as it was when you rented it. If you don't, you could end up paying for the difference (in a cleaning bill or a repair bill). If the production company should have to pay for your indiscretion, the company may not be as eager to hire you for the next job.

Location film crew and equipment trucks.

# PART FIVE
## ~Stage Versus Location~

© Miramax Films.  Director John Dahl on the set of ROUNDERS.  *Courtesy of Miramax Films.*

© Largo Entertainment. (Left to right) Bojesse Christopher, Director Kathryn Bigelow and Patrick Swayze, Keanu Reeves and James Le Gros on the set of the action-thriller POINT BREAK. *Courtesy of Largo Entertainment.*

# CHAPTER 16

## Stage Shooting

The general guidelines for obtaining production equipment and supplies were discussed in Chapter 12. This Chapter describes how your duties change when doing *stage shooting* ——the use of a sound stage for shooting the film or video. When shooting a commercial, the production company generally rents a stage for a number of days. If the shooting is to take place on stage, the sets to be used are built on the stage, the striking of the sets will take place on stage, and the wrap will be completed on the stage. Movies and television shows may rent or the studio may assign a stage for production; the sets may be struck, saved to be reused or permanment for that production.

The stage provides the location where the production will be shot, which means that all the production supplies and equipment go straight to the stage.  As you can probably guess, this arrangement makes your duties much easier than shooting on location.

The routines for stage shooting are the same as those for location shooting: deliveries, craft service, handling petty cash, and returning everything after the wrap.  (Remember that being early,  at least 15 minutes early is expected).  When prepping for a stage shoot, try to meet with the coordinator the night before the shoot.  At the meeting, discuss exactly what needs to happen in the morning at the production site.

Once you arrive at the stage and you have (a) delivered the camera gear, (b) set up the craft service (with the caterer), and (c)  delivered all the other production equipment, you are ready to begin helping everyone with every conceivable task —— all at once!  You can do it: Hustle, hustle, hustle. Much of the time, you may not even stay at the production site.  You may have to continue running all over the countryside dropping off and picking up equipment and supplies. Learn to take your frantic work style in stride.  You'll live longer and enjoy life more.

# CHAPTER 17

## Location Shooting and Signage

Preparing for the Shoot:

1. The day before shooting, you and the other Production Assistants and the Coordinator go over what needs to happen on location, including where things should be located.
2. The night before the shoot, you are responsible for charging (with batteries) the walkie-talkies, including an extra one to keep as a back-up in case something happens to one of them.
3. You will pick up all of the equipment (including the newly charged walkie-talkies) and load it onto the production truck (which is going to the location).
4. You production vehicle along one or two other vehicles may form a caravan to drive to the location.

## At the Shoot:

1. Once you arrive at the location (30-45 minutes before the rest of the crew), you will mark off the parking area for the production vehicles with a brightly colored parking cones.
2. You and the other PAs will set up a large sign with the production companys name and/or the name of the commercial show or film. The rest of the crew and the talent (the actors) will find the location based on your marking the parking area with the sign.
3. As the rest of the crew arrives, a Second AD (Assistant Director) or the lead PA will instruct everyone where to park. (Often, a police officer or fire fighter will be there to supervise).
4. You (and the other PAs) unload the camera gear, set up the craft service, help to unload everything as quickly and efficiently (but carefully) as possible. The walkie-talkies will come in handy when covering a large area. Start communicating, and start hustling right away.

NOTE: Though things are more spread out here than at the stage, the duties are basically the same as those spelled out in Chapter 12. Don't get caught standing around idly wondering what to do next. Go! Go! Go!

## Location Signage

As a Production Assistant you might be asked to help the Location Manager or if there is not one, guess who will be asked to hang or place signs (that you probably will have to make) to direct the crew to the location of the shoot. These signs are placed on street corners, usually with directional arrows. The crew follows this till they get to the designated location. Make sure they are secured into place, usually wire bailing wire.

Here are a few different methods and materials used for location signs:

## Method 1

Use a 20"x30" piece of foamcore, bright pink or bright yellow. Get a fat magnum black marker and hand print the name of the production company or initials or the name of the film or commercial with directional arrows. Do the same for the cast, crew, trucks etc. Secure the sign to the pole by punching two little holes from the middle out for the bailing wire. Secure the bailing wire to the pole or fence.

## Method 2

Use a 20"x30" piece of foamcore, bright pink or bright yellow. Print out from your computer on a normal piece of 8 1/2" x 11" white paper, the name of the production or initials or the name of the film or commercial with directional arrows. Do the same for the cast, crew, trucks etc. Then place that 8 1/2" x 11" piece of paper on the 20"x30" piece of foamcore. Secure the paper with scotch tape, clear 2" tape or by gluing it onto the foamcore. Secure into place using bailing wire.

## Method 3

Method three requires the use of a professional letter press on machine. These machines are used by professional sign companies. The machines have come down in price over the last five years and are affordable to the average person. More and more Location managers and Production Assistants are taking on these tasks. Here's how:

Use a 20"x30" piece of corraplastic (looks like corrugated cardboard but plastic), with a computer and a cutting arm for cutting out the letters from a roll of black vinyl, that you type into the computer (special software needed). Once you have finalized what is going onto the sign, hit send and the software sends the outline of the letters or picture to the cutting surface. Once the cutting is done, peel of the extra vinyl, then place the letters or picture onto the 20"x30" piece of corraplastic and press and hold for three to four minutes. The holes have rivets that you put in for the wire. It is a much more clear look and will withstand rain. This is plastic; the others are made from paper products.

Pictures of all three methods:

Method one.

Method two.

Method three.

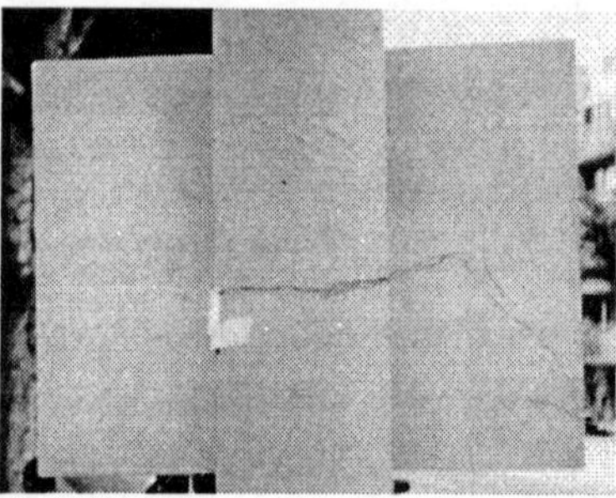
How to attach.

# PART SIX
## ~Money Matters~

© New Line Cinema, Inc. (Left to right) Renée Zellweger, Director Gary Sinyor and Chris O'Donnell on the set of the romantic-comedy THE BACHELOR. *Courtesy of New Line Cinema.*

© Columbia Pictures Industries, Inc. Producer/director Ivan Reitman (left) confers with Dan Aykroyd (center) and Bill Murray (right) on the set of the comedy GHOSTBUSTERS. *Courtesy of Columbia Pictures.*

# CHAPTER 18

## Getting Paid For Your Services

Two Methods of Payment

There are two methods of getting paid by the production company: via time cards or via invoices. The actual forms used signify a lot more that just a different piece of paper. *Time cards* are submitted by an employee to an employer——that is, the production company has hired you as a full-time or part-time, temporary or permanent employee. *Invoices* are submitted by an independent contractor to a production company that has contracted to purchase specified services, often only for a specified length of time, or for a specific job.

## Employees

When you are an employee, an entire body of regulations cover the ways in which your employer must treat you. One aspect of this is that the employer is required to deduct federal and state income taxes from your check before paying you. To determine the amount to deduct from your check, you are required to fill out an I.R.S. (Internal Revenue Service) W-4 form and an I-9 form. Also deducted from your check will be social security tax ("F.I.C.A."), but as an employee, the employer must contribute an equivalent amount to social security on your behalf.

If you are an employee, you must fill out a time card. On the time card, you must fill in your name, the job number, and the name of the production company for which you worked. If you are paid an hourly rate, you must carefully track the hours you work in order to record them accurately on the time card. If there is a space in which to record your hourly rate, fill that in. If, instead of an hourly rate, you are paid a flat rate, write "flat" on the time card, and record the amount of the flat rate. In either case, be sure to sign your time card at the end of the production or at the end of the week, whichever comes first, the production coordinator or  accounting personnel will take your time card. Most production companies pay employees on a weekly basis.

## Independent Contractors

The main advantage, for the production company, is that there are fewer goverment regulations, tax paperwork, etc.when they pay an independent contractor as verses an employee. Several other differences regarding status as an employee verses an independent contractor do not usually apply well to the PA job. For example, though independent contractors technically cannot be required to be at a specific work site during specific hours, the practical application of this may be impossible in this situation.

The major difference that applies to all independent contractors is the handling of taxes. As an independent contractor, you do not have taxes deducted from your check, and you are expected to pay estimated taxes each quarter of the year (April 15, July 15, September 15, and January 15). (If you neglect to pay estimated taxes, and owe income tax in excess of the prescribed amount, be assured that you will not only have to pay later, but you will also be assesed intrest and penalties for late payment). Also, you must pay both the employer's and the employee's share of social security tax, doubling your social security tax obligation. The Production Company doesn't pay social security tax for you, and they don't deduct your taxes from their payment to you, they still must report the money they give you to the I.R.S. For that reason, they require you to supply them with the correct information they need in order to report it accurately to the I.R.S. The following form illustrates what you might use. A simple form such as this provides all of the necessary information required by the production company when they report your payments to the I.R.S. Depending on the production company's requirements, you may be asked to file a federal form W-9 instead of or in addition to a self-contractor form.

As an independent contractor you must save all your receipts, proof of payments and keep track of your own expenses. You will need these documents to prepare your income taxes. For more information on being an independent contractor, get a copy of IRS publication 334, or consult the Small Business Association , a tax consultant or any relevant sources available to you.

## Payments (Wage)

Payments vary in different parts of the world. Independent PA's seem to earn the most per day on the West Coast of the U.S. (L.A. Hollywood). New York and Florida come in close behind Los Angeles. Union work, as an employee, has less variance. Outside the U.S., wages are slightly lower, adjusting for currency exchange rates and costs of living.

In areas outside major production centers, there is less union control and PA's, as with all crew members, earn less.

A good rate of scale for the L.A. area  is the following:
Independent (experienced 1 to 2 yrs.)- $125.00 to $150 a day.
Employee (staff-runner)- $250.00 to $325.00 a week.
New (less then 6 mos.)-$50.00 to $100.00 a day.

# SELF - CONTRACTER FORM

PAYEE _______________________________________

ADDRESS _____________________________________

_____________________________________

S.S.# / FED. I.D. # ___________________________

SERVICES RENDERED :



DATE: _______________________________________

RATE PER DAY : ______________________________

FOR PERIOD: ___________ TO __________ TOTAL $ ______________

I certify that this is a true and correct statement.

DATE: _________ SIGNED: ______________________________

CONTRACTOR

I certify the services listed hereon were rendered and approve this

invoice for payment.


DATE: _________ SIGNED: ______________________________

TITLE: ______________________________


DISTRIBUTION:          COMPANY NAME  REPRESENTATIVE


CHECK  NO: ___________          NAME: ___________________


P.O. NO: ______________          TITLE: ___________________

# Timecard

<table>
<tr><td colspan="3">Production<br>House Approval</td></tr>
</table>

Production Co.__________________________________

Employee Name____________________________

Soc.Sec. #____________________________________

Union________ Occupation __________________ Prep Wrap Shoot Code

| Job#<br>& Product | Date | Time in | out | Meals in | out | Rate | Str. | 11/2 | 2x | 21/2 | Other | Meal Penalty |
|---|---|---|---|---|---|---|---|---|---|---|---|---|
|  | MON |  |  |  |  |  |  |  |  |  |  |  |
|  | TUE |  |  |  |  |  |  |  |  |  |  |  |
|  | WED |  |  |  |  |  |  |  |  |  |  |  |
|  | THU |  |  |  |  |  |  |  |  |  |  |  |
|  | FRI |  |  |  |  |  |  |  |  |  |  |  |
|  | SAT |  |  |  |  |  |  |  |  |  |  |  |
|  | SUN |  |  |  |  |  |  |  |  |  |  |  |
|  |  | TOTAL |  |  |  |  |  |  |  |  |  |  |

For Payroll Use Only:

<table>
<tr><td>Form W-9<br>(Rev. January 2003)<br>Department of the Treasury<br>Internal Revenue Service</td><td>Request for Taxpayer<br>Identification Number and Certification</td><td>Give form to the<br>requester. Do not<br>send to the IRS.</td></tr>
</table>

<table>
<tr><td rowspan="7">Print or type<br>See Specific Instructions on page 2.</td><td colspan="2">Name</td></tr>
<tr><td colspan="2">Business name, if different from above</td></tr>
<tr><td>Check appropriate box: ☐ Individual/ Sole proprietor   ☐ Corporation   ☐ Partnership   ☐ Other ▶ .................</td><td>☐ Exempt from backup withholding</td></tr>
<tr><td>Address (number, street, and apt. or suite no.)</td><td rowspan="2">Requester's name and address (optional)</td></tr>
<tr><td>City, state, and ZIP code</td></tr>
<tr><td colspan="2">List account number(s) here (optional)</td></tr>
</table>

**Part I**   Taxpayer Identification Number (TIN)

Enter your TIN in the appropriate box. For individuals, this is your social security number (SSN). **However, for a resident alien, sole proprietor, or disregarded entity, see the Part I instructions on page 3.** For other entities, it is your employer identification number (EIN). If you do not have a number, see **How to get a TIN** on page 3.

*Note: If the account is in more than one name, see the chart on page 4 for guidelines on whose number to enter.*

**Social security number**

*or*

**Employer identification number**

**Part II**   Certification

Under penalties of perjury, I certify that:

1.  The number shown on this form is my correct taxpayer identification number (or I am waiting for a number to be issued to me), **and**

2.  I am not subject to backup withholding because: **(a)** I am exempt from backup withholding, or **(b)** I have not been notified by the Internal Revenue Service (IRS) that I am subject to backup withholding as a result of a failure to report all interest or dividends, or **(c)** the IRS has notified me that I am no longer subject to backup withholding, **and**

3.  I am a U.S. person (including a U.S. resident alien).

**Certification instructions.** You must cross out item **2** above if you have been notified by the IRS that you are currently subject to backup withholding because you have failed to report all interest and dividends on your tax return. For real estate transactions, item **2** does not apply. For mortgage interest paid, acquisition or abandonment of secured property, cancellation of debt, contributions to an individual retirement arrangement (IRA), and generally, payments other than interest and dividends, you are not required to sign the Certification, but you must provide your correct TIN. (See the instructions on page 4.)

<table>
<tr><td>Sign<br>Here</td><td>Signature of<br>U.S. person ▶</td><td>Date ▶</td></tr>
</table>

## Purpose of Form

A person who is required to file an information return with the IRS, must obtain your correct taxpayer identification number (TIN) to report, for example, income paid to you, real estate transactions, mortgage interest you paid, acquisition or abandonment of secured property, cancellation of debt, or contributions you made to an IRA.

**U.S. person.** Use Form W-9 only if you are a U.S. person (including a resident alien), to provide your correct TIN to the person requesting it (the requester) and, when applicable, to:

  **1.** Certify that the TIN you are giving is correct (or you are waiting for a number to be issued),

  **2.** Certify that you are not subject to backup withholding, or

  **3.** Claim exemption from backup withholding if you are a U.S. exempt payee.

  **Note:** *If a requester gives you a form other than Form W-9 to request your TIN, you must use the requester's form if it is substantially similar to this Form W-9.*

**Foreign person.** If you are a foreign person, use the appropriate Form W-8 (see **Pub. 515,** Withholding of Tax on Nonresident Aliens and Foreign Entities).

**Nonresident alien who becomes a resident alien.** Generally, only a nonresident alien individual may use the terms of a tax treaty to reduce or eliminate U.S. tax on certain types of income. However, most tax treaties contain a provision known as a "saving clause." Exceptions specified in the saving clause may permit an exemption from tax to continue for certain types of income even after the recipient has otherwise become a U.S. resident alien for tax purposes.

  If you are a U.S. resident alien who is relying on an exception contained in the saving clause of a tax treaty to claim an exemption from U.S. tax on certain types of income, you must attach a statement that specifies the following five items:

  **1.** The treaty country. Generally, this must be the same treaty under which you claimed exemption from tax as a nonresident alien.

  **2.** The treaty article addressing the income.

  **3.** The article number (or location) in the tax treaty that contains the saving clause and its exceptions.

  **4.** The type and amount of income that qualifies for the exemption from tax.

  **5.** Sufficient facts to justify the exemption from tax under the terms of the treaty article.

Cat. No. 10231X      Form **W-9** (Rev. 1-2003)

*Example.* Article 20 of the U.S.-China income tax treaty allows an exemption from tax for scholarship income received by a Chinese student temporarily present in the United States. Under U.S. law, this student will become a resident alien for tax purposes if his or her stay in the United States exceeds 5 calendar years. However, paragraph 2 of the first Protocol to the U.S.-China treaty (dated April 30, 1984) allows the provisions of Article 20 to continue to apply even after the Chinese student becomes a resident alien of the United States. A Chinese student who qualifies for this exception (under paragraph 2 of the first protocol) and is relying on this exception to claim an exemption from tax on his or her scholarship or fellowship income would attach to Form W-9 a statement that includes the information described above to support that exemption.

If you are a **nonresident alien or a foreign entity** not subject to backup withholding, give the requester the appropriate completed Form W-8.

**What is backup withholding?** Persons making certain payments to you must under certain conditions withhold and pay to the IRS 30% of such payments (29% **after** December 31, 2003; 28% **after** December 31, 2005). This is called "backup withholding." Payments that may be subject to backup withholding include interest, dividends, broker and barter exchange transactions, rents, royalties, nonemployee pay, and certain payments from fishing boat operators. Real estate transactions are not subject to backup withholding.

You will **not** be subject to backup withholding on payments you receive if you give the requester your correct TIN, make the proper certifications, and report all your taxable interest and dividends on your tax return.

**Payments you receive will be subject to backup withholding if:**

1. You do not furnish your TIN to the requester, or

2. You do not certify your TIN when required (see the Part II instructions on page 4 for details), or

3. The IRS tells the requester that you furnished an incorrect TIN, or

4. The IRS tells you that you are subject to backup withholding because you did not report all your interest and dividends on your tax return (for reportable interest and dividends only), or

5. You do not certify to the requester that you are not subject to backup withholding under **4** above (for reportable interest and dividend accounts opened after 1983 only).

Certain payees and payments are exempt from backup withholding. See the instructions below and the separate **Instructions for the Requester of Form W-9.**

## Penalties

**Failure to furnish TIN.** If you fail to furnish your correct TIN to a requester, you are subject to a penalty of $50 for each such failure unless your failure is due to reasonable cause and not to willful neglect.

**Civil penalty for false information with respect to withholding.** If you make a false statement with no reasonable basis that results in no backup withholding, you are subject to a $500 penalty.

**Criminal penalty for falsifying information.** Willfully falsifying certifications or affirmations may subject you to criminal penalties including fines and/or imprisonment.

**Misuse of TINs.** If the requester discloses or uses TINs in violation of Federal law, the requester may be subject to civil and criminal penalties.

## Specific Instructions

### Name

If you are an individual, you must generally enter the name shown on your social security card. However, if you have changed your last name, for instance, due to marriage without informing the Social Security Administration of the name change, enter your first name, the last name shown on your social security card, and your new last name.

If the account is in joint names, list first, and then circle, the name of the person or entity whose number you entered in Part I of the form.

**Sole proprietor.** Enter your **individual** name as shown on your social security card on the "Name" line. You may enter your business, trade, or "doing business as (DBA)" name on the "Business name" line.

**Limited liability company (LLC).** If you are a single-member LLC (including a foreign LLC with a domestic owner) that is disregarded as an entity separate from its owner under Treasury regulations section 301.7701-3, **enter the owner's name on the "Name" line.** Enter the LLC's name on the "Business name" line.

**Other entities.** Enter your business name as shown on required Federal tax documents on the "Name" line. This name should match the name shown on the charter or other legal document creating the entity. You may enter any business, trade, or DBA name on the "Business name" line.

**Note:** *You are requested to check the appropriate box for your status (individual/sole proprietor, corporation, etc.).*

### Exempt From Backup Withholding

If you are exempt, enter your name as described above and check the appropriate box for your status, then check the "Exempt from backup withholding" box in the line following the business name, sign and date the form.

Generally, individuals (including sole proprietors) are not exempt from backup withholding. Corporations are exempt from backup withholding for certain payments, such as interest and dividends.

**Note:** *If you are exempt from backup withholding, you should still complete this form to avoid possible erroneous backup withholding.*

**Exempt payees.** Backup withholding is **not required** on any payments made to the following payees:

1. An organization exempt from tax under section 501(a), any IRA, or a custodial account under section 403(b)(7) if the account satisfies the requirements of section 401(f)(2);

2. The United States or any of its agencies or instrumentalities;

3. A state, the District of Columbia, a possession of the United States, or any of their political subdivisions or instrumentalities;

4. A foreign government or any of its political subdivisions, agencies, or instrumentalities; or

5. An international organization or any of its agencies or instrumentalities.

Other payees that **may be exempt** from backup withholding include:

6. A corporation;

7. A foreign central bank of issue;

8. A dealer in securities or commodities required to register in the United States, the District of Columbia, or a possession of the United States;

Shown is the Form W-9 (2003) and partial instructions. Make sure you use the current form and read all of the instructions.

# CHAPTER 19

## Mileage / Vehicle Rental

As a PA, you are often required to use your own vehicle for many of the pick-ups and deliveries. You deserve to be reimbursed for the wear and tear on your vehicle. The best way to handle this is to go to the trouble of keeping a detailed *mileage log*. You can purchase a log or use something like the following:

| DATE | START MILES | END MILES | MILES TRAVELED | DESTINATION (NOTES) |
|------|-------------|-----------|----------------|---------------------|
| 8/22 | 35 | 55 | 20 | CAMERA RENTAL HOUSE |
|  | ------ | 100 | 65 | K.L EQUIPMENT |
|  | ------ | 120 | 85 | JJ ' s DONUTS |
| 8/23 | 150 | 160 | 10 | Location |

Not all companies require you to record all of your mileage, and some companies have their own mileage logs, but under no circumstances should you try to cheat a production company on the mileage you report. They have been in the business long enough to recognize when a mileage report is overly high, and a few extra dollars for mileage is not worth being fired (or never rehired) by a company.

Some companies prefer to rent your vehicle at a flat rate for the day or for the week. If so, they expect you to pay for the gas and other mileage-related expenses. If given a choice, however, you'll make out better with mileage reimbursement: it's worth the extra effort to record it accurately.

# APPENDIX 1

## Co-workers

This list, with brief descriptions should help you identify the job titles on a working set. (All of these titles may not be on every set.)

**Executive Producer**—Executive in charge of production. The senior financial or business production executive. Many times the title is granted for a major financial contribution.

**Producer**—The individual responsible for the creative shaping and final result of a film, television production or commercial.

**Line Producer**—A Producer who may work under an executive Producer, supervises most facets of production as well as the work of the production manager.

**Associate Producer**—An assistant to the Producer. Can be a production associate with responsibility for a specific area of production or an elevated title for a production department head e.g., Associate Producer in charge of Casting. There can be several Associate Producers on any one production.

**Director**—The individual responsible for realizing the intentions of the producer and the script; specifically in control of on set action and dialogue in front of the camera.

**Assistant Director (AD)**—The person who carries out number or procedural duties for the director, which include scheduling shooting, calling personnel, maintaining order on the set, checking budgets, rehearsing performers, coordinating with the front office and doing whatever tasks the Director may find necessary.

**Second Assistant Director**—The person who marks the slate and claps the sticks on the clapboard before each shot. This person is also responsible for loading the magazines.

**Director of Photography (DP)**—This person is in charge of the technical requirements for lighting and photographing the production. The creative DP will also consult and assist the Director in scenic composition, technical mood, choice of camera angles, and camera set-ups.

**Cameraman**—The person who operates under the Director of Photography and is directly responsible for managing the camera during shooting.

**Assistant Camera (AC)**—The person in the camera crew who is responsible for proper maintenance of the camera during shooting. As well as checking that the camera works properly, this person is responsible for changing lenses and magazines and following focus during shooting.

**Production Manager**—The individual in charge of the daily business arrangements for shooting. He or she starts out by calculating an economical way to employ equipment, performers, locations and properties. The Production Coordinator arranges for transportation, accommodations, and meals and hires extra personnel as needed.

**Art Director**—The person responsible for the design and overall physical appearance of the world in which the actors appear. He may design and oversee the construction of the setting.

**Costume Designer**—The person who designs and coordinates the clothing worn by the characters in the production. The Costume Designer works in coordination with the Director, Art Director and sometimes with the Director of Photography.

**Set Designer**—The person who designs and draws the plans and writes the various specifications for each set or setting.

**Set Decorator**—The individual who decorates or dresses the set with props, furnishings.

**Wardrobe**—The person responsible for getting clothing, costumes, and accessories for the production before the actual shooting begins and for maintaining them during the actual filming.

**Property Master**—The individual responsible for obtaining, altering, or building properties and making sure they are available when the filming is to begin.

**Gaffer**—The head electrician in a film production, who is responsible for ordering, placing, operating and maintaining the required lights as well as the power source. The gaffer has a number of electricians working under him or her.

**Best Boy**—The assistant to the Gaffer.

**Key Grip**—The head of this department. Responsible for an assortment of jobs. A Grip does an assortment of hard jobs and must have a "grip" while carrying or pushing the dolly.

**Grip**—The assistant to the Key Grip.

**Sound Mixer**—The person in charge of recording sound during the actual shooting of the production.

**Boom Operator**—The sound technician who operates the boom and the microphone attached to it.

**Script Supervisor**—The individual responsible for maintaining perfect continuity from shot to shot by keeping a record that specifies individual takes and their details.

**Teleprompter Operator**—The person responsible for the cuing device placed near the camera with rotating scroll so the performers can read their lines.

**Casting Director**—The individual who chooses and negotiates contracts for the performers.

**Make-Up**—The person responsible for applying make-up to the performers in the production.

**Home Economist**—The person responsible for preparing the food for the on camera shooting.

**Stylist**—The person who takes care of the hair of both the female and males performers.

**Special EFX**—The person in charge for the effects achieved through special photographic techniques or processes and those specifically created before the camera when it is shooting.

**VTR Operator**—The person responsible for recording the image and sound on tape for playback on a television system.

**Location Scout**—An individual who goes in search of suitable places, either indoors or outdoors, for a production that is shooting on location.

**Location Manager**—An individual who contracts for their use and arranges the details of occupancy.

**Craft Service**—The personnel in the production that performs tasks such as food, coffee, and snacks for the crew and performers.

# APPENDIX 2

## Glossary

These terms that will help you on the set and around the industry.

**Aces and Deuces**— The power of light. Aces are 1K or 1000 watts of light and Deuces are 2K or 2000 watts.

**Acrylic Sheet Filters**—Are used outside windows to correct for color temperature of daylight to tungsten light or tungsten daylight. They are usually 4"x8" and are heavy to carry.

**Action**—When a Director od an Assistant Director calls "Action" it means start the activity being filmed.

**Alligator Grip**—This is a spring loaded lighting grip used to attach a light to pipes, molding and doors.

**Ambient Light**—Light that exists or naturally occurs in a scene.

**Aperture**—The opening gererally controlled by the diaphragm, that regulates the amount of light to pass through the lens and reach the film.

**Applebox**—Wooden crates used to elevate tables, stands, performers, etc.

**Arrifflex**—A brand name of 35mm and 16mm camera made by a German company.

**Artificial Light**—The light created for a scene, that comes from an electrical source.

**Avid**—A company that builds digital non-linear editing equipment.

**Backdrop**—A large painted scene on cloth or on a flat, often seen through a door or window.

**Background Action**—Subsidiary action taking place at the same time as the major action.

**Backlight**—Light coming from behind a subject and in the direction of the camera. It serves not illuminate but to define the edges of its subject.

**Back Lot**—The area of studio ground where outdoor sets are built for exterior shooting.

**Barn Doors**—A unit made up of two or four hinged doors that is attached to the front of a lamp to direct the light source.

**Bead Board**—4"x 8" sheet of foam approx. 1" thick

**Behind the Scenes**—The off-camera goings on associated with filmmaking.

**Below the Line Expenses**—All physical production costs not included in the above the line expenses, including material costs.

**Blacks**—Any fabrics used to block out light from windows and doors, during the day to give the appearance of night.

**Blocking**—Planning the positions and movement of the performers in a scene.

**Bluescreen**—A process whereby actors work in front of an evenly lit, monochromatic (usually blue or green) background. The background is then replaced in post production with stock footage or computergenerated images, to form the background.

**Bolex Camera**—A lightweight hand held 16mm camera made in Switerland.

**Boom**—A long, mobile, telescopic are with a microphojne attached at one end that is held over the speaker's voice.

**Boucelight**—Lamps aimed at walls and ceiling to create diffuse light.

**B-Picture**—A cheaper made, less ambitious and less publicized film.

**Budget**—The total amount of money to be spent on a production, calculated in advance by the company.

**Call Time**—The time you should be on the set. Remember! If you're on time your 15 minutes late.

**Call Sheet**—A listing of which crew and actors are required to perform and or work on the production for that specific today and time.

**Cast**—A collective term for the actors appearing in a film or commercial.

**Camera**—The basic tool of all cinematography for photographing a series of progressive images on a strip of film.

**Camera Car**—A car or truck specially designed and fitted to carry one or more cameras as well as people.

**Camera Angle**—The placement of the camera in relation to the subject of the image.

**Camera Right/Camera Left**—These directions are from the camera's point of view. When facing the camera your right is the camera's left.

**Camera Report**—A list of scenes from the script that have already been filmed, or a list of the contents of an exposed reel of film stock.

**Camera Speed**—The rate per second of frames exposed in the camera.

**Camera Tape**—Tape similar to duct or gaffer's tape, comes in 1" wide rolls, mostly used by Camera Assistant to reseal cans after they were opened.

**Camera Wedge**—A device placed upon the tripod to support the camera and allow for greater angles of tilt.

**Can**—A metal or plastic circular container for storing film.

**Catwalk**—A narrow, railed walk suspended above the stage in the studio.

**Changing Bag**—A lightproof bag with two linings, two zippers, and sleeves on each end through which hands may extened to load film into, or unload film from the magazine.

**China Pencil**—A grease pencil used in editing for marking up the work print with instructions and many other uses.

**Chicken Coop**—Alluminaire with six one-thousand watt bulbs which is covered in the front by wire mesh, used as an overhead light.

**Chromakeying**—An electronic and or computerized technique that allows for specific color elements to be replaced with different picture elements.

**Clapboard**—A slate with a pair of boards hinged together that is photographed at the beginning of each take. On the slate are written name of the project, Director, date, and scene number.

**Clean Speech**—A take in which all dialoque was performed without error.

**Clear the Frame**—An order to vacate the set in front of the camera during rehearsal.

**Close Up**—A shot in which the subject is larger than the frame.

**Continuity**—Is the proper matching of details, movement and dialogue from shot to shot.

**Core**—A plastic hub of two or three inches in diameter on which film is stored.

**Cookie**—Is a cutout piece of pattern, cut out from a material and placed in front of a light to cast a patterned shadow.

**Craft Service**—Responsible for maintaining a table of snacks between meal times.

**Cue**—The signal given to an actor to begin a speech or action.

**Cutaways**—Shots done away from the main action.

**Cutting Room**—The room where the film is edited.

**Cut**—Stop all the action.

**C Stand**—A metal stand the grip uses to hold flags.

**Dailies/Rushes**—The first positive prints, usually synchronized with sound, which generally are delivered by the laboratory the day after shooting.

**Dissolve**—An editing technique where the image of one shot is gradually replaced by the image of another.

**Ditty Bag**—A small canvas or leather bag that contains tools, tape, wire, etc. that a person might need on the job.

**Dolly**—A mobile platform on wheels that supports the camera, allowing the camera to move.

**Doorway Dolly**—A dolly narrow enough to pass through standard doorways.

**Double**—A person filmed in place of a lead actor when a stunt is too dangerous or to relieve the actor from tedious technical set-ups.

**Drop**—A large, heavy canvas like black cloth. Usually used to blacken out windows.

**Emulsion**—The layer of light-sensitive silver salts, suspended in gelatin, which is coated on the base of film.

**Exposed**—The state of film when it has already been used in the camera.

**Extra**—An actor hired to appear in a crowd scene. They are hired day to day and receive no credit for their performance.

**Fade**—A gradual means of closing or starting a scene, indicates a break in action or time, or place.

**Feet Per Minute (FPM)**—The speed with which film passes through a camera.

**Film Stock**—The physical medium on which photographic images are recorded.

**Fire Up**—To start any equipment.

**First Unit**—The primary crew for a film production as opposed to second unit.

**Flags**—Metal frames with a rod on the end and covered in black cloth to cut light.

**Flare**—A fog or glow over the image, generally caused by some strong light directly hitting the lens of the camera.

**Flat**—A wooden frame covered with muslin, wood, etc. and used for scenery or as a back drop.

**Floating Wall**—A part of a wall in a set that can be removed to allow for movement of the camera.

**Focus**—The sharpness of an image, or the adjustments made on a camera necessary to achieve this.

**Fog Machine**—A portable device that can be carried by hand or placed on the ground to make controlled amounts of fog or smoke.

**Footage**—The measure of the film in feet.

**Foreground**—The front area of a scene closest to the audience, where the major action takes place.

**Frames Per Second**—The number of frames that pass before the aperture of a camera per second.

**Framing**—The act of fitting a subject into the frame for photographing.

**Freelance**—Any person who is independent and is not contracted to a specific production company.

**From the Top**—The Director's comand to start a scene from the beginning.

**FX**—Abbreviation for effects used to represent such terms as sound or special effects.

**Gate**—The part of a camera supporting the pressure plate that holds the film, on track behind the lens.

**Gaffers Tape**—2" wide cloth tape looks like duct tape.

**Gear Labels**—Temporary labeling of walkie talkies. Pre-cut cloth tape labels 1" x 3", 60 on a roll. www.gearlabels.com

**Gel**—A transparent cellophane material; used for changing the color of light.

**Generator**—A motor-driven machine that creates electricty as an additional source of energy for lighting a studio or location.

**Greensman**—The person responsible for trees, shrubs, etc. on a set.

**Grip Chain**—A lightweight chain used by the grip to fasten down an assortment of jobs.

**Grip Clips**—Small, medium, large metal reusable clothes pins.

**Grip Truck**—A small or large truck rented by grips to transport equipment or props.

**Half Apple**—A wooden box, half the height of an apple box.

**Hand Model**—A individual whose hands alone are photographed.

**Hand Props**—Small items such as books, pens, cups, cards used by performers during shooting.

**Head Shots**—A shot in which the frame is largely taken up with the head of the performer.

**Hit the Juice**—A direction to turn on the electricity for lights for shooting.

**Honeywagon**—Mobile trailer/vehicle with restrooms for location shoots away from soundstages.

**Hot Set**—A set all prepared for shooting, with scenery and props in exact position and lighting for use. The set should not be entered while hot or with Red Light flashing.

**Houselights**—The general lights in a stage or studio exclusive of those used on the set for filming.

**Independent Film**—A motion picture made by a filmmaker who has no connection with the Hollywood scene.

**In-House Unit**—A production unit that belongs to the company rather than one hired for a single production.

**Independent Producer**—An individual who produces independently and is not under contract to a studio or production company.

**Insert**—A close up shot of an object, often produced by the second unit, inserted into the final version of a film or commercial.

**Insert Stage**—A small studio employed for photographing close-ups of objects that will be inserted into the commercial or film.

**Interior**—Indicates that the scene occurs indoors.

**In Shot**—Any person or object accidentally in a shot.

**In the Can**—The term that the shooting of the entire project is finished.

**Juicer**—Slang for a electrian.

**Kill**—To turn something off.

**Lab**—The place where film is developed and printed at the various stages of the production.

**Layout Board**—A thin piece of cardboard that comes in 4"x 8" sheets, used to cover a surface to save it from being marked up.

**Layout Board Rack**—A metal or wood rack that is placed into a production rental truck to hold the sheets of layout board.

**Lens**—An optical device used by a camera to focus an image onto film stock.

**Live Action**—Events in a production performed by living people as distinguished from those performed by animated fiqures.

**Load**—To place unexposed film in a camera or camera magazines.

**Location**—Any place other then a studio where a production is in part or completely shot.

**Lock It Down**—A direction given by the assistant director for everyone on the set to be quiet. It is call prior to the rolling of the film.

**Lot**—The outdoor area of a studio where sets are constructed or stored and where filming sometimes takes place.

**Low-Budget Production**—The making of a production with limited amount of money.

**Magazine**—A light-proof container that feeds the film into the camera.

**Magic Hour**—The brief period of dawm and dusk that allows enough light for shooting.

**Martini Shot**—The last shot of the days shoot.

**Matte Shot**—A photographic technique where artwork and live action are combined.

**Motion Control**—A camera set-up which records the motion of a camera during a shot so that visual effects can be synchronized with the photographed scene.

**MOS**—Initals printed on a clap board and appearing at the start of a take to indicate that the scene was shot without sound.

**Moviola**—A portable machine to screen dailies and edit film. www.moviola.com

**Nagra**—A synchronous tape recorder used in the industry.

**Natual Lighting**—The term is most often used to describe daylight or illumination from the sun.

**NG Take**—A take which is "no good" and not usable.

**No Print**—An instruction on a camera report to the lab that a certain take should not be printed.

**O.K. Takes**—Takes that are satisfactory and should be delveloped.

**On Camera**—Any object or performer visible in the cameras field during shooting.

**Out Take**—A shot ont used in the final version of the project.

**Pan**—The action of rotating a camera about its vertical axis.

**Parallels**—Portable scaffolding to elevate camera or lighting equipment.

**Picture Car**—A vehicle shown in a film or commercial.

**Pick-Up Shot**—The shot taken from a point where the previous shot has ended.

**Playback**—The playing of images, and often sound from a videotape that have just been recorded from the scene.

**Point of View**—A camera angle in which the camera views what would be visible from a particular objects position.

**Print It**—The order given by the Director when he or she is satisfied with the take.

**Production**—This term refers to the phase of film/commercial making during which principal photography occurs.

**Production Report**—A daily report of actual progress as well as notes regarding on set activities of the cast and crew.

**Production Schedule**—A detailed plan of the timing of activities associated with the making of a film or commercial, usually handled by a production manager.

**Promo**—An abbreviation and a slang for "promotion" which means a type of publicity for a project.

**Prop Box**—A container with smaller props needed for a days shooting.

**Red Light**—The camera is rolling. Wait for the red light to stop flashing before entering the stage.

**Reel**—A strip of film wound on a metal wheel.

**Reload**—To place another film magazine in the camera or tape in the recorder.

**Retake**—To reshoot a scene because the previous take was unsatisfactory.

**Reverse Shot**—A shot taken at a 120-180 degree angle from the preceding shot.

**Room Tone**—Different sets and locations have different audio characteristics. A sound recordist will typically make a recording of the natural ambient "silence" on a set or location; he or she will us it as a reference point.

**Roll Camera**—The order from the Director or Assistant Director to start the camera.

**Safety Shot**—A second shot of a scene made for insurance in case the previous shot might be faulty.

**Sandbag**—A heavy canvas bag filled with sand, used to support equipment at the base.

**Scene**—A continuous block of storytelling either set in a single location or following a particular character.

**Scene Dock**—The place in a studio where parts of a set used for scenery are stored.

**Scratch**—A mark or cut in the form of a thin line that appears on the emilsion or base of a film.

**Second Unit**—A small unit of film technicians, subsidiary to the principal film unit.

**Set**—An artificially constructed place for the action of the film or commercial.

**Short End**—The unexposed film that remains in the magazine of the camera after shooting because it is too short to use for another complete shot.

**Shot Composition**—The arrangement of key elements within the frame.

**Shot List**—A list of all the shots in the order in which they were photographed during filming.

**Showcard**—Comes in 32"x40" cards. It is used to bounce light off of and for cue cards.

**Shutter Speed**—The length of time that a single frame is exposed for.

**Silk**—A diffuser, made of a stretched piece of white material on a frame.

**Slate**—The recorded identification of scene and take numbers, usually done with a clapboard. Most takes are identified at the beginning a "tail slate" marks the end instead.

**Soft**—Unsharp images, doesn't sharply define the objects.

**Sound Stage**—A special studio/stage for shooting and recording sound for a film or commercial.

**Spaghetti Western**—A western filmed in Italy.

**Spec**—Working for free or for anticipated future payment.

**Speed**—An announcement made by either the director of photography or camera operator indicating to the director that the camera is operating at the correct speed.

**Spool**—A plastic or metal cylindrical device on which is wound with flanges on the sides of the spool protecting the edges of the film.

**Squib**—A small explosive device, which, when detonated, will simulate the effect of a bullet/puncture wound or small explosion.

**Source Book**—Is your personal book of the names and phone numbers, people, production companies, rental houses, etc., that you have acquired over a period of time.

**Stock**—Unexposed film also referred to as raw stock.

**Storyboard**—A sequence of pictures created by a production illustrator to communicate the desired general appearance on camera of a scene.

**Swing Gang**—Personnel from the film crew who work at night readying the set for the next days filming.

**Sync**—A term used in film that relates to synchronized sound and picture.

**Tag**—The final scene on a film or commercial, after the climax, that ties up all the action.

**Take**—A single continuous recorded performance of a scene.

**Tails Out**—This term refers to a reel of film or tape with the end on the outside.

**Tail Slate**—The slate that marks a shot at the end of the take instead of the beginning.

**Telecine**—The process of transferring images from film to a video signal, including frame rate and color corrections.

**Tilt**—The action of rotating the camera either up or down.

**Timecode**—Electronic guide track added to film, video or audio material to provide a time reference for editing, synchronization.

**Track**—A single component or channel of a soundtrack.

**Tracking Shot**—The action of moving a camera along a path parallel to the path of the object being filmed.

**Trailer**—An advertisement for a film which contains scenes from the film.

**Thread Up**—To position film so that it will run properly in its path through a piece of film machinery.

**Tripod**—A three-legged support for the camera made of hard-wood or stainless steel.

**Two-Shot**—A medium close-up of two subjects, usually framed from the chest up.

**Upstage**—The rear part of the stage

**Visqueen**—Plastic that comes in different thickness, usually clear or black. Used to cover equipment and things.

**Walk-Away**—Leave the set and or stage, a "wrap" is not required, filming will resume the following day.

**Wedges**—A piece of wood 10"x4"x 1/16" tapers to 1" thick.

**Western Dolly**—A transport for a camera during shooting that can carry a heavy load.

**Wild Track**—A sound track not recorded in synchronization with the shooting of a scene.

**Wild Sound**—Scenes that are filmed without the sound being recorded at the same time.

**Working Title**—The name by which a movie is known while it is being made. This is sometimes different from the title with it is released.

**Work Print**—A print made from the original negative. This is what is picked up at the lab, the next day for screening.

**Wrap**—The completion of the productions shooting for that day or for the entire film or commercial completion.

**Wrong Set**—A term indicating that a set is no longer needed for shooting, and that it is time to start shooting on the next set.

# APPENDIX 3

## National Film Commission Offices

| | |
|---|---|
| Alaska Film Commission | 907-269-8120 |
| Alabama Film Comission | 800-633-5898 |
| Arkansas Film Commission | 501-682-7676 |
| Arizona Film Commission | 800-523-6695 |
| California Film Commission | 323-462-6092 |
| Colorado Film Commission | 303-620-4500 |
| Connecticut Film Commission | 860-571-7136 |
| Delaware Film Commission | 302-739-4271 |
| Florida Film Commission | 877-352-3456 |
| Georgia Film Commission | 404-656-3591 |
| Hawaii Film Commission | 808-586-2570 |
| Iowa Film Commission | 515-242-4726 |
| Illinois Film Commission | 312-814-3600 |
| Indiana Film Commission | 317-232-8829 |
| Kansas Film Commission | 785-296-4927 |
| Kentucky Film Commission | 502-564-3456 |
| Louisiana Film Commission | 225-342-8150 |
| Massachusetts Film Commission | 617-973-8800 |
| Maryland Film Commission | 800-333-6632 |
| Maine Film Commission | 207-287-5703 |
| Michigan Film Commission | 800-477-3456 |
| Minnesota Film Commission | 612-332-6493 |
| Missouri Film Commission | 573-751-9050 |
| Mississippi Film Commission | 601-359-3297 |
| Montana Film Commission | 800-553-4563 |
| North Carolina Film Commission | 919-733-9900 |
| North Dakota Film Commission | 701-238-2525 |
| Nebraska Film Commission | 800-228-4307 |

New Hampshire Film Commission                603-271-2665
New Jersey Film Commission                   973-648-6279
New Mexico Film Commission                   800-545-9871
Nevada Film Commission                       702-486-2711
New York Film Commission                     212-803-2330
Ohio Film Commission                         800-230-3523
Oklahoma Film Commission                     800-766-3456
Oregon Film Commission                       503-229-5832
Pennsylvania Film Commission                 215-686-2668
Rhode Island Film Commission                 401-273-3456
South Carolina Film Commission               803-737-0490
South Dakota Film Commission                 800-952-3625
Tennessee Film Commission                    615-741-3456
Texas Film Commission                        512-463-9200
Utah Film Commission                         801-741-4540
Virginia Film Commission                     804-733-2403
Vermont Film Commission                      802-828-3618
Washington Film Commission                   206-956-3200
Wisconsin Film Commission                    800-345-6947
West Virginia Film Commission                304-458-6657
Wyoming Film Commission                      307-235-9325

# APPENDIX 4

## Film Unions, Television Unions, Film Guilds and Television Guilds

ACTRA Alliance of Canadian Cinema TV & Radio Artists—Canada
800-387-3516
AEA Actors' Equity Association  212-869-8530
AFL-CIO America Federation of Labor  202-637-5000
AFM American Federation of Musicians  323-462-2161
AFTRA-SAG Dallas/Ft. Worth  214-363-8300
AGMA American Guild of Musical Artists  212-265-3687
BECTU Broadcasting Entertainment Cinematograph & Theatre Union
UK—British Actors' Equity  020 7379-6000
CFTPA Canadian Film & TV Production Association
800-656-7440
DGA Directors Guild of America  800-421-4173
DGGB Director Guild of Great Britain UK  020 7278-4343
IATSE International Alliance of Theatrical Stage Employees, Moving Picture Technicians, Artist and Alliance Crafts of the United States, Its Territories and CA  212-730-1770
IATSE East Coast Council  212-730-1770
IATSE Local 1 Theatrical Stage Employees  212-333-2500
IATSE Local 212 Calgary, Canada  403-250-2199
IATSE Local 302 Projectionist & Video Technicians, Alberta, Canada  403-282-8267
IATSE Local 363 Nevada  775-786-2286
IATSE Local 600 International Cinematographers Guild
323-876-0160
IATSE Local 700 Editors Guild  323-876-4770
IATSE Local 829 United Scenic Artists  323-965-0957
IATSE Local 839 Screen Cartoonists  818-766-7151

IATSE Local 839 Screen Cartoonists             818-766-7151
IATSE Local 876 Art Directors                  818-762-9995
IATSE Local 884 Studio Teachers                310-652-5330
IATSE Local 891 Canada                         604-664-8910
IBEW International Brotherhood of Electrical Workers
                                               202-883-7000
IBT International Brotherhood of Teamsters      202-624-6800
NABET Local 700 Canada                         416-536-4827
SAG Screen Actors Guild                        323-954-1600
WGA East Writers Guild of America East          212-767-7800
WGC Writers Guild of Canada                    800-567-9974

## THE THEATRE PROPS HANDBOOK  by Thurston James

A step by step guide to the design and construction of theater properties.  This practical, profusely illustrated handbook explains the use of materials essential to the props builder and demonstrates the techniques involved in the construction of more than one hundred specific property items.  Emphasis is placed on safety of construction and use of props, particularly those which use electricity or simulated fire.  An updated, detailed appendix lists sources for all the materials referenced in this book.          **272 pgs.  PB   8.5x11   0-88734-934-X**

## THEATER PROPS WHAT WHERE AND WHEN
### by Thurston James

A unique reference source that describes and illustrates a comprehensive variety of items, from the common to the obscure, placing them in the appropiate historical period and describing their proper functions.  Ideal for stage, film and television production.  Invaluable for designers, directors, prop builders, actors and writers.
**192pgs.      PB   8.5x11   0-88734-935-8**

## STAGECRAFTERS HANDBOOK          by I. E. Clark

A clear concise handbook detailing the responsibilities of each member of a Theatre Technical crew.  Not a How-to but a What to do!
**96 pgs.  PB   5.5x8.5   0-88734-649-9**

## CORRUGATED CARDBOARD SCENERY
### by Bryant H. Lee and D.M. Wedwick

A comprehensive, profusely illustrated and detailed workbook on how to use cardboard for theatrical design and construction.  Written in a comfortable, easy to read style so that anyone involved in the design of props, sets, costumes and even puppets will be able to easily use this as a step-by-step guide.
**192 pgs.  PB   8.5x11   0-88734-628-6**

## PRINCIPLES OF STAGE COMBAT HANDBOOK
### by Claude D. Kezer

Punches, kicks and knock-outs...whips, swords, and knives... Learn it all, from your first fall to your first stabbing. Learn to behead, beat, and battle with the ease of a professional. A safety first guide. Don't get murdered without it!          **96 pgs.  PB   8.5x11   0-88734-650-2**

## SCENERY                                              by W. Joseph Stell

Design and Fabrication of theatrical Scenery. This practical, profusely illustrated textbook thoroughly explains the process of developing a scenic design concept and provides technical information on scenery, construction, painting and rigging. "...insightful and thorough descriptions of the design process...wonderful line drawings..." CHOICE

**256pgs  pb  8.5x11  over 200 photos and illus. ISBN 0-88734-663-4**

## THEATRE MANAGEMENT
### by Suzanne Celentano and Kevin Marshall

This is a hands-on, guide to producing and theatre management. It is a comprehensive view into running a profit/non-profit theatrical venue. The book is designed with both the novice and experienced producer/manager in mind. Includes financial, administrative, marketing, legal, producing a show and much more!

**208pgs  photos 8.5x11 pb    ISBN 0-88734-684-7**

## COMEDY WRITING WORKBOOK                  by Gene Perret

Sharpen your comedy skills with Bob Hope's head writer! Perret shares the success secrets of dozens of all-time great comics from Phyllis Diller to Woody Allen, from Jack Benny to Robin Williams. Not only will you be able to write and create jokes, but you will increase your abilities for comedic scripting and performing. You might become a unique comedian.

**192 pgs  pb   8.5x11  ISBN 0-88734-647-2**

## THE AMERICAN MUSICAL THEATRE
### by Steven Porter

An indispensable guide for student or professional. It is a history, production blueprint, guide to criticism, and source of projects. An ideal workbook for student, writer or critic, actor or director, producer or teacher. Important for any Musical Theatre Library.

**128 pgs  pb  8.5X11  0-88734-686-3**